GET
NAKED
WITH
ME

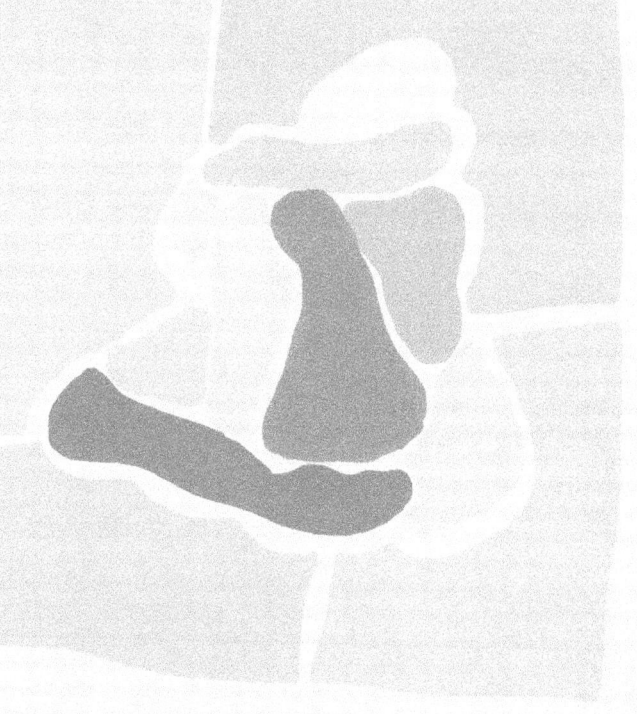

Also by the author

NOVELS
  2018 Do You Really Know Camille?

POETRY
  2016 About a Girl: A Poet's Journey to Love and Enlightenment

  2018 Bloom

COOKBOOK
  2022 Dish

GET NAKED WITH ME

by Sharon Jeter

cooper broadwater publishing
RALEIGH, NORTH CAROLINA

Get Naked With Me
Copyright © 2020 by Sharon Jeter

Cooper Broadwater Publishing, Inc.
Raleigh, North Carolina
www.coobropub.com

All Rights Reserved.
Printed in the United States of America
First edition January 2020

If you would like to use material from this book,
Prior permission must be obtained by contacting the publisher.
Thank you.

Write to Permissions:
Cooper Broadwater Publishing, Inc.
604-1011 East Front Street
Clayton, NC 27528
coobropub@gmail.com

ISBN 978-1734501810 (paperback)

Acknowledgements

It's never too late for reinvention.

Thank you to all the boss women, that through your tireless navigation of this rough and tumble world, have allowed me to realize the possibilities and know that I am not done yet.

To Mom, June, family, friends, and my precious little Buddy, thank you for loving me so fiercely.

*...everything is like the rose,
prickly and sweet*

content

Introduction .... *xi*

Accomplice 1
Ah 2
Ain't Nobody Gon Know 2
An Inside Job 3
Anchored 4
Another Minute 5
Baby Girl 6
Back To Okay 7
Be Like The Breeze 7
Black Folk Coping 8
Blame Game 10
Breathless Glory 11
By Invitation Only 12
Certainly 13
The Chirper's Revival 14
Chocolate Cake 15
Closer To Being 16
Compassion Now 16
Corrective Punctuation 16
Crumbs 17
Crying A Blues 18
Crying, For All Of You 19
Crystal Clear 21
Daddy Should Have 22
Despite Everything 26
Directions 27
Double Check 28
Dying To Change 29
En Garde 30
Endings 31
Enough 31
Eve & Apples 32
Everything Is Temporary 33

Fair Warnings	34
Fast Times	35
Foolish	36
Foolish Heart	36
Forgiveness	37
From The Front Porch	38
Get Naked With Me	39
Get To It	40
The Gift	41
Girl In The Mirror	43
Go Be Great	44
Good Morning Sunshine	45
Goodbye To Everything	46
He Smiles	47
His Name Was Carlos	48
Holding On	50
Home In Autumn	51
Hope	52
Hope Possibly	53
I Am Too	54
I Believed You	55
I Knew Love	56
I New	56
I See, You See	57
I Still Love	58
I Try	59
I Was Just Remembering	60
I'm Hot	61
I'm Still Me	62
I'm That Woman	63
Intoxication	65
It Was A Woman	66
It's Over Now	67
It's True What They Say	68
It's You	69
Just Maybe	71

Just One Of Those Days	73
Kissed	74
Knowing Love	75
Lemonade	76
Light	77
Like Oxygen	78
Looks Like Rain	79
Loved Too	80
Maybe Not	81
More Than A Dream	81
Morning Juxtaposition	82
My America	83
My Beautiful Surrender	86
My Mystery	87
My Tears Are My Strength	89
New Me	89
No Instructions Necessary	90
No More	90
No More Rose	91
No Regrets	92
Not Enough	93
Not Now	94
Offerings	95
Oh, Wretched Bitterness	96
On Exercise	97
On Getting Naked	98
On Pebbles	99
Pebbles And Stones	99
Popcorn Ceilings	100
Possible	101
Precious Peace	102
The Road	103
Role Model	104
Same Ole Me With You	105
Seasons Are Changing	106
The Shirt	108

Sometimes	109
Spilled Milk	109
Soul Meet	110
Still	111
Still Soul Dreamin'	111
Substantiated Cry	111
The Sun Will Shine Again	112
Sweet Betrayals	113
Sweet Sax	114
There, Their, They're	115
Think It Through	115
Thinkin'	116
Time Has A Way	118
Today	120
Touch Up Paint	121
United, Well Stand!	122
Violin	125
Wait A Minute	126
Wait To Free	127
What I Like	128
What Is This	129
What To Do	130
When You Know	131
Where We Left It	132
Why I Shine	133
Wish	134
Within	135
Woman	135
Woman Power	135
You Are	136
Your Worst Enemy	137
The Breakdown	139
Accomplice	*141*
Ain't Nobody Gon Know	*142*
Anchored	*143*
Another Minute	*144*

Breathless Glory	146
Crying, For All Of You	146
En Garde	148
Endings	149
From The Front Porch	150
Good Morning Sunshine	150
Goodbye To Everything	151
I Believed You	154
I Still Love	154
I'm Hot	155
It Was A Woman	156
It's Over Now	156
Lemonade	157
Maybe Not	158
New Me	158
The Shirt	159
The Sun Will Shine Again	159
Sweet Sax	159
There, Their, They're	160
Where We Left It	160
Your Worst Enemy	161

INTRODUCTION

I'm putting it all on the table in *Get Naked With Me*. By the time you finish this book you're going to know all my business. I don't know why I'm doing this to myself, but these words just had to come out, they simply couldn't be contained.

These poems speak to the children I never had. Words I would tell my own daughters and sons, if I'd given birth. My life of course, inspired these works. Some are love psalms, some are about family, some about friends, and some about nature and culture. And although they were inspired by different events, they serve as a snapshot of a moment in time that evoked raw emotion.

The poems in *Get Naked With Me* are arranged alphabetically so there isn't a chronological progression to follow that parallels my personal evolution. Towards the back of the book, I provide backstory for some of the poems.

I did it this way because I have taken classes before where an entire semester was dedicated to trying to analyze what the writer was thinking when they wrote a particular phrase. I found such speculation ridiculous, because unless an explanation was provided by the author, no one would ever know, not really. All the presumption in the world is just wasted time and energy.

One of my favorite poems in this collection *is, It's Over Now*, p. 67. I read this poem almost every day, hoping its words will infuse into my soul and force me to live in the moment and let go of the past, let go of what I hoped for, just plain let go. I'm a work in progress but thank God I'm better than I used to be.

Many of the poems in *Get Naked With Me* were first published in 2016's *About a Girl: A Poet's Journey to Love and Enlightenment* and 2018's *Bloom: New and*

Selected Poetry. After feedback from colleagues and friends, asking what inspired this or that, I decided to take some of the most popular poems and include them in this book with a narrative to explain.

I chose not to include many of the 'I love you so much' poems, as I am so far removed from those feelings and the relationships that inspired them, that focusing on them felt antiquated, deciding instead to let those works speak for themselves.

The poems in *Get Naked With Me* are emotional, raw, funny and amusing. You'll connect with some of them and question the merit of others. But by the end, you will know me completely, heart and soul.

Enjoy!

GET NAKED WITH ME

by Sharon Jeter

accomplice

Your eyes have seen it
You know it exists
Yet you sit silently
And do nothing as chaos persists

No hand in the plan
Or knowledge thereof
In fact, disgust, you feel the emotions
Just the same as us

Though power is your friend
And you can affect change
Despite all this, you take no blame
Yet indecision makes you an accomplice,
    unnamed

The fairness of your complexion
The consequence of your birth
Renders your inaction unfortunate
Stunting progress,
And choking the breath out of
    this great nation

So, until you surrender
And act against this unrighteousness
Standing up for the unseen,
    the unheard,
        the overlooked,
            the cries of your neighbors
You are an accomplice
Who, with full knowledge,
Cozies up to injustice,
    to racism,
        to murder,
            to lies and deceit

To all the things you claim to abhor
And that's what makes you just as guilty,
    just as responsible
As the perpetrator

ah...

Ah is a full sentence
That doesn't need to be explained
If you've ever overcome or experienced pure bliss
You know exactly what it means

ain't nobody gon know

Ain't nobody gon know
I can just tell them what they wanna hear
Am I gon do what I need to do, for me?
Or am I gon just sit on my ass again, right here?

Ain't nobody gon know, but me
They stopped questioning me long ago
Guess that means they've figured me out
That I'm an idle fool still teetering, in limbo

Ain't nobody gon know, but me
But what I'm finally starting to understand
Is that it doesn't matter who else knows, out there
If I'm not accountable to this soul within

an inside job

I must apologize to you
And to myself
I was angry and resentful
For a long, long time
Because you wouldn't give me what I wanted
What I thought I needed
But what I know now
Is that I have to be…
Everything I wanted from you for myself
I have to be the peace I long for,
    the love I desire
I have to carry all this within me
And become peace
Become love
For me, alone
So, when I don't get it from you
From out there
I'll have enough already
Inside of me
No more anger
Because you couldn't see me
No more fighting
To get what I already possess
Now that I stand here
Whole and complete
All by myself

anchored

Our souls have called out,
One to the other
Both answering at this precise moment in time
Now that we have found each other,
What do we do?
Unready in a multitude of ways
Yet desiring true love
And craving affection and acceptance
Do we yield to our yearnings?
Being inept as we are
Or do we surge on
Preparing our hearts and minds
For the things that our limited capacities
    will surely fail to deliver
I say, YES!
Absolutely
Submitting all that I am and have to you
My worthy King
And you gladly do the same
Supporting me as your Queen
Trusting in the hopes of the heart
That together we can overcome our weaknesses
And build a future of forever
Anchored by love

another minute

I wish I had another minute
Or hour, or day, or week
A chance to see things, different
To know you tenderly

I wish I had another minute
Or hour, or day, or week
Not time to just waste again
But to cherish each moment completely

I wish we had another minute
Or hour, or day, or week
To make sure we could feel
How much we mean to we

I wish we had another minute
Or hour, or day, or week
All the time desired and needed
To right our history

BABY GIRL

We said our final goodbyes
And I swore I wouldn't cry
After all, I never knew him
He was a stranger whose blood I shared
We stared our last stare
Standing, as we spoke for the first time
He said, "I'm sorry baby girl.
I never told you that I'm sorry
I didn't know how to
But not a day went by
Not one day of your life
That you weren't on my mind,
Baby girl."
Maybe next time
I always dreamt of that moment
The one where we would talk
I longed for time,
Just daddy and me
Now, I have all the time in the world
It seems
And I heard him
I felt him, for the first time
He said,
"Baby girl, I love you."
And that's not all
"Please, forgive me
I did the best I knew how to do"
And that was that
The last time I saw my daddy
Was the first time I truly saw my daddy

And I'll always be his baby girl

Back to Okay

After all the rain I allowed
Accepting ordinary
With this time apart
And breathing
Just breathing without you
It's hard to go back
To being okay with you
Especially since
I'm finally fine in my solitude
Constantly wondering why
Why would I go back
Why I stayed so long
Why I ever agreed,
To all of me and only part of you
And now my needs stand guard
Making memories of my wants
And I am okay once again
I'm finally back to okay

Be Like the Breeze

I want to be like the breeze
Carefree and ease, see
Me flowing a gentle sigh
Touching the world dancing, by
The way I was there
Blowing leaves through the, air
Cooler oh so slightly though
Not like the gusting wind, no
Just a breeze

BLACK FOLK COPING

Bang Bang…Damn!
They shot again
It's blue and it's you
Y'all killing em'
But we're not laughing
We're outraged, this sarcasm
Just black folk coping

Doleful and anxious
These lives denied
Their chances to bloom
And yet you're consumed
Cause I don't look like you
Ridiculous, but it's still true
Just black folk coping

And when one in three
Black men in this society
Are incarcerated
And children see this as their destiny
That there's no other way
Is what they'll say to themselves
Just black folk coping

Where's that dream
The one hoped for by a King
And all of our ancestors
Whose spirituals sung, sang, sing
In our ears, freedom's ringing
Can you hear it, we're not
Just black folk coping

There's so much more to us
Then we even know ourselves
We can hardly contain it

Our unexpected infectiousness
We are pure authentic bliss
And silly you, thinking we're
Just black folk coping

Blame Game

Don't blame the storm clouds
For wanting to cry
Or the sorrow to come
When bidding goodbye

Don't blame the sun
For shining so bright
Or the stars in the sky
For twinkling at night

Don't blame the broken hearted
For needing time to mend
Or tossing caution aside
Heedlessly trying again

And don't blame love
For being bittersweet
Or restless time
For marching on incessantly

There is no blame
For not knowing the truth
Or even when it lay bare,
Allowing fickle feelings to choose

There are many, many things
That truly warrant blame
But what is the use
It won't change a thing

BREATHLESS GLORY

I want my life to reflect the way I feel right now
This goldilocks weather bringing me to tears
Breezes tiptoeing through my hair
    in spurted gusts
Causing displays of puffery in my clothing
I look out with inspired attention
Smiling, totally welcoming more
Marshmallow clouds sail on by
Forming familiar shapes off in the distance
It doesn't really matter that I don't know their names
They greet me with kindness anyway
Have you ever seen a more brilliant blue
Than the one spanning the distance as far as the eye
    can see
And I want to sway in the rippling gentleness of the waves
Somehow, I feel they will carry me to where I belong
Then I notice the magnificent giant
Slowly retreating off to the west
Leaving behind a spectacle of deliciousness
And I beg to be its companion
Because I know that even with guaranteed goodbyes
It will always return, shining
Awe!
I want to stay here forever
In this moment blooming with dreams
In this feeling of breathless glory

BY INVITATION ONLY

You were not invited
So I was wondering why you even showed up
How you ever got in the door,
I do not know
But you came in like
I had left the door wide open
Just for you
You made yourself comfortable,
In my abode
Propping those size thirteen shoes
On my brand-new coffee table
Almost looked like you owned the place
But why are you here
Interrupting my party
Smelling so good
And smiling at me with those…
Ooohh…
Gorgeous white teeth
So I repeat, 'this party is by invitation only'
Flashing that degree and all those credentials
Won't stop me from asking you to leave
So don't even bother,
I've heard it all before
And though your body is saying more to my femininity
Then your mouth ever could
I still ask…
'Do you have an invitation?'
'No,' you respond
With that do I really need one, I'm Mr. Right smile
Mistakenly thinking my heart will listen
To your delightful gibberish
'This party is by invitation only,' I say one last time
And escort your fine *@% to the door
With no hesitation at all

Certainly

I like this
I hate this
It's what I want
I want no part of it
And I'm not confused at all

I'm happy when I see you
Please get out of my face
I want you to call
We talk way too much
And this is exactly what I desire

Your love is sweet
You need to kiss me
Your touch, oh
I want no more
I'm completely sure without a doubt

You know what I mean
I feel all these things.
I love you
I do….
Certainly!

THE CHIRPER'S REVIVAL

Melodious ballads that I try to understand
An orchestra of distinctive songs
Soloists, piccolos adrift, various flautists whistling
I'm not at all certain about this though
That's just what it sounds like
Chirp, chirp…
    Squeak…
        Tweet…
            Cheep, cheep…
Even a knock, knock, knocking on wood
What are they all abuzz about, I wonder
Wanting desperately to join the choir
To imitate, in total adulation
Squawk…
    Squawk…
        Squawk…
I chime in
Hoping they'll sing along with me
But I'm out of tune
And not quite as sweet as their
Chirp…
    Squeak…
        Tweet…
           Cheep, cheep…
But now I'm a part of the revival,
A part of the glorious composition
And somewhere in the midst of our mighty sing-along
I began to soar, too

Chocolate Cake

Uummmm…
I love chocolate cake
You look so succulent
Delicious!
And although I haven't had cake in a while
I must have some of you
To resist you any longer is impossible
You please ALL of my senses
And entice me to do things I know I shouldn't
In your presence my mouth waters uncontrollably
You just look that damn good to me
Daily I resist my desires to taste you
For I know with just one taste
The insatiable binge will begin
Foolishly I ponder of your goodness
In vain I avoid your site
Because once my mouth indulges in your mocha essence
My tongue will start its dance
And I won't be able to stop until you're finished
When my mouth is filled with an explosion of delight
Then, just to ensure that I haven't wasted a single drop
I'll lick my contented lips and my fingers too
I won't deny myself your pleasures anymore
I must savor your flavors
And reward myself with a piece of you

Uummmm…
I love chocolate cake

CLOSER TO BEING

The further I move away from you
The closer I get to becoming...

COMPASSION NOW

Could not comprehend
Then one day it touched my life
Now I empathize

CORRECTIVE PUNCTUATION

Never good with punctuation
Biased toward commas and semicolons
When periods were clearly necessary
Allowing for far too many details
Prolonging stories meant to be short and sweet
Into novels
And many times, sequels
Editing was often ignored
But repetition has forced awareness
Now, the errors that were once overlooked
Are made of crystals
And I add corrections where needed
Long before the consequences of inaction
Result in the disappointment of an exclamation mark!

CRUMBS

Crumbs always leave you wanting more
And are only good if you've already devoured
The thing that generated them
Or if you're hungry
So, no sir
I don't want your crumbs
Your leftovers
What remains
After you've already given the rest of you
Your time, your love, your money, your heart away
Save it for the next hungry fool
Been eating crumbs too long
They never satisfy
Not even a little
And for the greedy
I have no crumbs for you
They've all been sopped
It's just that good
Nothing left for the wanting
Not even conversation

CRYING A BLUES

I am crying a blues
Why, you ask
It's simple, you see
A metamorphosis is happening
An awakening
So, I cry
A blues for the girl
I now know
'Cause from this day on
That girl is no more
However sad
It's so amazing too
The transformation that will occur
And if by chance
This change interrupts
Your plans for her life
Oh well
You can cry a blues too
But the girl of yesterday
From this day on will be
All new
For what was and for what's yet to be
I am crying a blues
A blues for her
She is me

CRYING, FOR ALL OF YOU

I cry for you Philando
For all of You,

Where I feared for my life was enough
Enough to take yours, a not guilty
Enough to leave your children fatherless
Enough to break your mothers' hearts
Enough for reasonable doubt
I wonder if this would work for us
Cause we definitely fear being black motorists

I cry for you Philando
For all of You,

Killed, stopped for a broken taillight
Seven shots, it's just not right
I was afraid for my life, is what they'll say
The words that they use to persuade
Their false reality, it's a shame
Killed for the blackness they couldn't change
And all the stereotypes projected upon us

I cry for you Philando
For all of You,

Cause unfortunately this is not happenstance
These shots are still blasting again and against
That's why we cheered for the acquittal in ten
Nineteen hundred and ninety-five, oh man
Feeling a small piece of justice
In a system that's stacked high against us
Against us, for simply being black

I cry for you Philando

For all of You,

Who didn't deserve to die this way
When will you get your justice
Now that we are all witnesses
What can we tell our children
So that they won't end up victims
To these, our modern day lynchings
And we're still protesting, on our knees, with fists

So, I'll continue to cry
For you Philando Castile
And for all of You,
Who didn't deserve this death
For all of You,
Who'll never get justice

Crystal Clear

You don't know me
Because of this
I'm gonna give you just one pass
And offer some good advice…
Keep walking
Shut up, you loudmouth
Stay out of my business
And leave me alone
Cause I'm bout due to let just the right person have some of this
So, unless you're ready
I would kindly suggest that you be on your way
Don't misconstrue my silence
I'm not at all meek or humble
And I don't mind unleashing all of this frustration on you
Heed this warning,
Because you don't know me
But if you're feeling yourself, keep it up
I dare you

DADDY SHOULD HAVE

You should have shown me what love looks like
What love feels like
But you left me to fend for myself
I guess you were too busy
Preoccupied with what ever
Your own mess
So instead you gave me away to the men of the world
Allowing them to teach me what you should
    have shown your little girl
So today I choose to forgive you
And let go of the hope of forty years
I feel it's my responsibility to let you know
You should have told me
So that I could grow
Up to be a strong black woman
Not always searching for what love looks like
And I wouldn't have had to learn it from just any John Doe
Daddy you should have shown me,
    so that I would know
What real love looks like
You should have been there when I was three
Showin' momma love
Instead of hiding behind the door
Scaring us like crazy
And when you thought we were sleep
You should have left mom alone
But we heard you
And I cried
Part of my soul must have died
That night
And then when I was six
Playing with pixie sticks
When momma was out working
And grandma was gone

Aunt Mary was doing her thing
So, I was left at home
With a family friend
You should have been there for me
The lessons I learned in that house
Were never meant for any child's eyes to see
And at thirteen
I often wondered where you were
Robbed of my innocence
Left alone
Again, momma was working
Big brother was gone
Away to school
The Beve and I became one
Such a fool I was
I thought it was fun
In my twenties while searching for love
A baby was conceived
I didn't know how to deal
With the responsibility
And never wanting
My baby to long for love from its dad
The love I didn't know
With regret I let my precious go
I wish you had shown me what love looks like
Daddy I wish you had known how to show me
What love looks like
Oh, how I wish you had known
I'm certain had you possessed this knowledge
You would have given it to me
And for all the johns and jehs and them
That pushed me away when they were done
    doing what they do
Although it was them that threw me away
In my eyes it was always you
On my wedding day

When it came time to give me away
The deed had already been done
You see
You gave me away when I was three
When you and mom separated
Not knowing what to do
You left
In my heart, I now know you did the best you
    knew how to do
I wish you had known
What your daughter would need
When you wonder why I don't call
How I look through you like you're nothing at all
You should have shown me
It was your job to do
Momma was doing the best she could
Never once did I see her with a male friend
Although it was best for us kids
I didn't see how she related to men
What I needed from you
You should have told me that I was a beautiful little girl
When the world showed me differently
I would have known
And especially when the men
They came calling
If these words I would have heard from you
I wouldn't have longed to hear them so badly
And when trouble packaged in a lovely body
Spouting enchanting words
I wouldn't have so easily swayed
Daddy you should have shown me
But you didn't know
Did you
I can't be mad at you anymore
For not doing something that you didn't know how to do
Daddy,

But how I wish you knew
I wish you could have been that strong black man
The one your little girl needed
Just maybe,
I'd be free

Despite Everything

I am amazing…
    despite many flaws
    and not yet realizing my full potential
I am persisting…
    despite stumbling repeatedly
    and constantly wanting to just give up
I am succeeding…
    despite the systemic constraints of racism
    and those who are biased against my curvaceous
        splendor
I am prospering…
    despite the societal limitations on gender
    and sexual orientation
I am beautiful…
    despite what you say about my kinky mane
    or think of my colorful Kente
I am loved…
    despite all the hate
    and the many times I've been hurt
I am graceful…
    despite failing repeatedly
    and resisting the inevitability of change
I am light…
    despite the darkness
    and all the despicable things I've seen
I am resistance…
    despite any sign of advancement
    or feeling like I am in this struggle all alone
I am life itself…
    still learning, still growing, still flourishing
    despite everything

DIRECTIONS

A step at a time,
One by one,
We'll all go our separate ways
Never again to realize
The memories of these days
We're on our own to go about
And make of ourselves what we shall
To be the best at everything
Hoping never to fail
The future for us is unknown right now
And in time will be uncovered
We'll work our hardest,
And be our best,
It will soon be discovered
Some goals of ours
May be unreachable
Fantasies they are
The path to which we want to go
Sometimes seem so far
Tomorrow will come, you'll see
Everything will be all right
New goals we shall seek
With new directions in sight

DOUBLE CHECK

Toothpaste
Check
Toilet tissue
Check
Soap
Check

Heading to the checkout

It looks like Christmas in here
Damn

Frustrated
Waiting in this long line

Reading magazines
Uhm…he died again
Laughing at absurdities

Getting close now
Then,
Finally,
I'm next

Dang,
Forgot the batteries
The double A's
Can't do that

Back at the end of the line
Again
Reading headlines
Again
This time happily waiting

DYING TO CHANGE

One of life's guarantees is that change will come
Reluctance can't prevent it
Only delay the inevitable
And even wanting,
    there will be challenges
Reminders of who we used to be
Our discarded versions of brokenness
That people fighting surrender won't let you forget
Though inconsequential to the masterpiece being
    sculpted
Only relevant to illuminate the distance between now and
    then
In awe that the unrecognizable stranger
    was once one in the same
Even in contemplation,
Remain steadfast to this ever-evolving newness
Knowing that each tomorrow
Can be vastly different than all the yesterdays
And when realizing the limitless possibilities ahead
Burst into a hallelujah celebration of pure unabashed bliss

en garde

The date has been set
A duel of sorts, arranged
A wise woman
Experienced in the ways of war, advised
The Samurai would never go to battle without his sword
Expecting not to fight
Even if a truce had been agreed upon
The enemy speaking words that equate to peace
Will be well prepared for combat
In which case, there are but two choices
One, the outcome guaranteed
Abandon the fight
With this you'll live to see tomorrow
And can strengthen your forces
And prepare your mind
The second choice
The outcome uncertain
Defeat, a possible conclusion
But then again, so is victory
Is the opposition a worthy tryst?
If choosing wisely, refrain
Odds being not in favor of a longing heart
Or a body desirous of contact
Knowing that in weakness
I have recently fallen to another
With my current opponent
Touting his persuasive skills
Not confident in my own
I'll believe his vain words
And heed the advice of the wise one
Forfeiting this battle to win the war
And fight again another day
Fully braced

endings

You slapped me with your callous words
I stayed,
Pouring everything I had into you
Into the façade of us

You crushed me with disrespect
And I stayed,
Broken,
But still pouring

You beat me down with betrayals
But I still stayed,
Gradually, waking up
I began to let go of us, deliberately

Learning how to love, just me
Setting myself as the only priority
For the first time
Instead of you, instead of us

Finally, it's over
I'm never looking back, not again
Happiness became my new lover
And that is where I stayed.

enough

My eyes have seen him
My breath is gone
But only a glance
Yet enough to satisfy all of me

eve & apples

I thought I really liked apples
But this internal fire sucks
Not to mention the rollercoaster ride of emotions
I don't know about way back then
But apples just ain't that good for all this
Eve, I know we family
But girl, we need to talk

everything is temporary

I had a revelation today
Though sad, it's wonderful too
Everything is temporary
And although I knew this
Although I knew the words
I never really knew until this very moment
Changing how I comprehend the world
Why, you ask
Because sometimes we try desperately
    to hold on to things
        to people
            to love
                to situations
When their time has passed
We cling to the emotions
    to the memories
        to the feelings
That these things gave us
Grasping desperately
Trying to hold on to things that are fleeting
Is like attempting to capture air in your hands
It simply can't be done
But we still yearn to hold on to these temporary things
Because we ache for the sensations that they gave us
Thinking only about our lives in that instance
Mistakenly believing we'll never feel
    or have
        or do in quite the same way again
But my darlings, time moves on
We drift to the next momentary thing
That's just the way it is
Life is all about inviting and dismissing experiences
So, holding on to those things
Thinking that they are forever

    is a waste of time
Nevertheless, it's essential to embrace everything
Feel everything
Learn from each and every experience
All the while knowing,
    knowing,
        knowing with certainty,
That everything is temporary

Fair Warnings

If you remind me of anything
That hurt or took time to heal
I'm turning around, crossing the street
And running like Forrest Gump
It's that simple, now

Fast Times

Last year I was five years old
Making mud pies
And playing with baby dolls

Six months ago, I learned to write in cursive,
In Mrs. B's 3rd grade class, kissed a boy behind the house
And got my period on my eleventh birthday

Just one month ago in high school
I got drunk, fell in love the first time, earned that diploma
And said goodbye to everything familiar

Last week I graduated from college
Landed a colorless job, got married, had those 2.5 kids
And we even bought that house with a picket fence

We were living the dream, obviously
The kids grew up, friends moved on, our parents passed
And we learned to love each other all over again

Now I'm pausing, hot and cold
Older than yesterday but not old
And I'm dreaming about you, my beloved

You were yesterday's everything
Now kissing your cold lips farewell, life was good
And it all flew by so, so fast

FOOLISH

Foolish of me
To believe you when you said
I love you girl
Foolish of me to believe
You could be different for me
Then you've ever been before
Foolish to know
And pretend to not know
That was foolish
And now it's done
No more questions left to answer
No more tears to shed
Now that my eyes have seen the truth
Of what my heart already knew
I feel so foolish

FOOLISH HEART

I have been a fool
Said he loved, but he didn't
Clarity can hurt

Forgiveness

I was firm in my delivery
And my words were met with understanding
I forgive you
Repeating for clarity
I forgive you
Never will I allow your callous mistreatment again
Co-conspirator
I accepted beneath that which I deserved
No more
I say no more
Yesterday matters not
The tears form
Looking at my reflection
The offender of the afflictions
Me

FROM THE FRONT PORCH

I can't see the sun anymore
It's hiding behind the homes across the street
It's not dark quite yet
But house by house, the lights began to flicker
On,
Then off,
Then on again,
And off again
The birds are still chirping
But soon they grow quiet, too
Little by little
Nature's exchange,
The crickets start to serenade
A thousand alternating foot rubs
The neighbors return from their Easter celebration
    with kind greetings
A mosquito flutters
Missing, but not giving up
The dog relaxes at my feet
And I notice the pollen,
Still gathering on the cars
The grass will need tending to soon,
But not tonight
The neighbor's hydrangeas have blossomed
Painting the landscaping,
    in bubblegum, magenta and cobalt,
Faintly sharing a pungent sweetness
I see the first stars of the night
Soon they all make an appearance, like popcorn
The gradual chill ends tonight's performance
Silently applauding, I stand in ovation
For the view from the front porch

Get Naked With Me

My wildest desire
I cannot deny
Is to be naked with you
And if by chance you know not what I mean
I shall take a moment to explain
You see I am sure
That bare nakedness would be good
No clothing
Not that
You've misunderstood
Without a doubt in time
That will be
But first
You've got to get naked with me
So, when I say
I want to see you in the nude
Please note
I am not talking about your manhood
Nooooo
That's easy to see
I'm asking you
Please
Just get naked with me
What I'm speaking of
Lies beneath what's seen
I'm talking
True
In · to · ME · see
I want to say who I am
And be what I dream
I want to be Real with you
I want to be REAL
I just want to take off all these clothes
To you, I want to be exposed

I want to share my fears
And my desires
And be comfortable knowing
My secrets,
They'll go no farther
I want to be able to cry
When feeling overwhelmed
And know to you
I can turn when I need a friend
Around you,
I want to dance
In my non-rhythmic way
And laugh and sing
Without caring
But caring all the same
The most awesome gift
That you can give to me
Is to allow me to be naked
And to get naked with me

Get to It

Dying
That's easy
We all will do it
Now, living
That's the challenge
Go, get to it

THE GIFT

Such joy
Me with you
Ecstasy barely describes
You departed
Forlorn
Darkness ensued
Unlimited time
Contemplation endless
Tears and sadness
Constant companions
Oh, so gradual
In cessation
Slowly the rain
Returns to a drizzle
Dark clouds
No more
And the sun reveals
A revelation
The gift
Of you
Crossing in time
My path
Still
Only a student
I am awakened
Attention anew
Insight immeasurable
Once just yellow
Now sunshine
Not only green
But radiant emerald
Brilliant
No
Extraordinary

Not just love
But me
A love
So intense
For me
You gave me
A gift
And for that alone
I thank you

GIRL IN THE MIRROR

There's a mirror in the bathroom
It's just above the sink
Positioned precisely
So that every time I get out of the shower
And pull the shower curtain open
Just for a moment or two
Looking into the steam covered mirror
I see myself as a little girl
The one in the photograph taken so many years ago
I have the same bowlegged form
In the photo, I am wearing my mother's bra
Stuffed full of socks
And sporting that Angela Davis wig
You know the one that was commonplace back in the day
I can see myself in mamma's heels
Standing there, miss sassafras
With my hands on my little girl hips
Leaning slightly to one side
Smiling
Oblivious to anything but my own cuteness
Looking into the mirror
Sometimes I reminisce
And while drying off
I have to laugh at that little girl
She hadn't a clue of what the world could do
There was no telling her she wasn't cute
Or that she could never do this
Or accomplish that
That little girl believed everything was possible
So now whenever pessimism stares at me
Making me doubt what I know to be true
I am always comforted by the warmth of a shower
But mostly,
When I open the shower curtain

And I am taken back to the memories of that little girl
The one who believed in everything
And doubted nothing
I can face my reality with a new resilience
A new steadfastness
Looking in the mirror
For a brief moment, I remember
Everything is possible
And I am grateful for the little girl in me
The one I see in the mirror

Go Be Great

Be better than me
And I was pretty damn good
Your greatness awaits

GOOD MORNING SUNSHINE

All the times I missed you
Almost fifty, every day since
Been thinking I was here alone
And then I got your kiss

I awoke early just to see you
You retreated last dawn
Hello, I smile at your appearance
You've been here all along

Deep breath to clench the moment
A memory lovingly embraced
Reluctantly, I depart
But grateful, you smiled on me today

GOODBYE TO EVERYTHING

Tonight, I'm settling all scores *(in my Godfather voice)*
And I'm saying good riddance
Dying, you could say, to everything
Everything I knew
And everything I used to be
Saying goodbye to my backward ways of thinking
To people who meant me no good
To those I used to call friend,
That took and took, giving nothing in return
And I was ripe for the receiving
Receiving of love, of kindness, of knowledge
Tonight, I'm saying goodbye to stagnate relationships,
That had no chance of being more
To dreams that never came true
To unhealthy opinions about myself and others
I'm saying goodbye to the hope that things could have
    been any different than they were
To people whose ignorance went overlooked
    for far too long
To the lies I believed about love
I'm releasing all the negativity and angst that
    came with chasing what was never meant for me
And I'm renegotiating the terms of my life
Only asking for and accepting what I want,
And what I deserve
With these firm declarations, I am yet afraid
Fighting the reluctance of familiarity
Though determined to never look back, again
With the foresight that the future is sprinkled with
    uncertainty
I still shout a resounding WELCOME
To all the new adventures awaiting

My freedom is in goodbye

He Smiles

Is God happy when I cry?
I wonder
I'm doing a lot of crying these days
I wonder if He rejoices at the sight,
Or if He delights
Cause He knows it means I'm maturing
I bet He smiles when I cry
Knowing it is time,
That I am ready to be better, do better
God, keep smiling at my tears
Cause You know one day I will listen
And then,
I will be the one smiling

His Name Was Carlos

His name was Carlos
He was as smooth as chocolate milk
Everything about him
Really
But what's smooth at that age
Whatever
He was
He was white chocolate
Decadent at best
Skin as luscious as silk
His eyes
The color of emeralds
And a smile that only sunshine could dare compare
Oh, he was all that
And to me
More
He was my first
And I hazard to say
Although some have followed
He was the only
He was me
And I
I was in love
Though brief our encounter
Three years
Maybe four
Through him
My life was forever changed
But you see
I had to leave him
And the pain caused by that separation
Akin to labor
At life's inception
And my life at that time was just beginning

You don't hear me
Although of age
I was being reborn onto my next journey
A journey on which he would not be a part
And in time
Like the leaves changing color in autumn
Gradually he ceased,
To hold my heart
And my mind captive
And in time
When the leaves all had fallen from the trees
Winter arrived as it does
And so did another him
Gone was Carlos but along came Tim
He loved me for what love was at twenty-three
But when I loved him back
He took his love from me
Only significant
Because
My comeuppance he was
You see once this man
Once he hurt me
I sought my revenge
And to this day I regret my carefree ways
For how I treated him
Those days I did pay
My payback came by the name of Jeh
No need to recollect
It's all the same
I didn't love me
And invited in the rain
And it came
And it came
Until I decided to change
And now
Not needing

I'm free
And I'm in love with me
But every now and then
I think about Carlos
He was my first
Love

HOLDING ON

At the end of my rope
Wanting,
But not wanting to let go
So, I held on
And cried
As my fingers reluctantly released
Familiarity allowed for complacency
Although the truth always accompanied the journey
Not easily ignored anymore
In the darkness
I embraced it, deliberately
Finally, tired and ready

Home in Autumn

Going home in autumn
Is like spending time in heaven on earth
All cares slowly dissipate with every westward mile
The mountain air refreshes the senses
Coercing careless forgetfulness
Eye to eye with blazing burgundies, rustic tangerines,
Sparkling crimsons, and mustard golds
Whispers of change inevitably unfolding
A look over the wandering hilltops
And you can see eternity right from where you stand
The endless winding roads beckon excited breaths
I think this is where life began
Where a slight breeze twinkles between your toes
And the cloudless blue-sky smiles
Making radiance your companion
And encouraging conversations
With strangers you'll never see again
Fallen leaves crunch beneath your feet
And you're forced to take steps you never planned
The sun sets surprisingly without notice
As the spectacular surroundings glow in the moonlight
You find yourself fighting with the crisp evening air
In hopes of capturing one lasting peak
There is a renewed awe of this place I call home
And I'm in love with Asheville all over again!

Hope

I am here

Sitting in this ole chair
A reupholstered heirloom
Much, much older than me
Looking around this bedroom
It is in desperate need of a renovation
Regretfully, I realize
That I am the room
And I begin to reminisce
On love
And on melancholy
On twenty years of memories
Written all over these neglected walls
Fresh from the dryer
A down comforter is folded across my lap
I wish I were like the dog
Unaffected by any of this mess
Effortlessly finding contentment
In his new home atop the plushness
Ours is a bond I never sought
But appreciate, now
Both of us just sitting here
Quietly listening
Then I hear a drip, drip, dripping
And I exhale in relief
Realizing it's coming from outside
The sound of the sun
Smiling again
As the first winter's snow melts
It trickles off of the rooftop
And for this alone, I am grateful
Just grateful
Though I still don't know

How to fix all this brokenness
I am ecstatic at the revelation
That there wasn't another mountain

HOPE POSSIBLY

I had so much hope
For love's possibilities
That's why I'm crying

I am too

I am a tree, centuries old
Leaves flowing in the breeze
I reinvent myself with the seasons
Transforming as I please

I am lavender and chamomile
Sweet and sublime
I can calm the senses
And sooth the mind

I am a wave in the ocean
Carrying you away
Strong and powerful
Yet gently I ripple by the bay

I am mother to many
A child to some
I am a sister and a cousin
Enemies, I have none

I am a teacher and a student
A seedling yet to bloom
Constantly looking in your mirrors
I am my own womb

I am novel and ripened
Naïve in many ways
Many things I have yet to experience
Yet I am wise beyond my age

I Believed You

Used to be,
I could pretend
Make up stories of how I wanted things to be
Tell myself that I was just fine
Not knowing
Not seeing you
But that was all lies
Couldn't even convince my own self
The silent whispers of a grown woman
A little girl lost
Then occasions unfold as they do
Time no longer agreeing to play along
In my make-believe world
And all the pain that I thought was gone forever
Blew me away, a roaring hurricane
If only I could do it all over again
I'd tell myself a different story
One that included
The lyrics uttered with labored breaths
'I have always loved you'
Allowing your words to infuse into my little girl soul
And for the first time I could be whole
Not needing or looking for love anymore
Because I believed you
And I'd know, it was real

I Knew Love

A new love
A really real, true kinda love
Only once
But I knew it

One where I didn't have to ask if
No pinching myself
Never!
That's how I knew
The question marks didn't exist
Not ever, ever, ever, EVER!

And I knew that once
　…upon a time

Wish I had realized it then
I wish that I had appreciated it
When it was in my grasp
And that's why hindsight is a bitch

But what can be done about that now
But to live in the memory
That I was adored
That I once walked as one with love
And that alone all by itself was worth it

I new

I knew I was loving me some me
When I decided to resist the temporary pleasures
Of certain people, situations and things
Knowing that they would eventually cause pain

I see, you see

I see white
You see right
But that ship won't sail

You see blue
I hear boo
And I'm scared as hell

I see shots
You say it's not
But someone's dead

You see strength
I feel angst
And I'm scratching my head

And this is just the beginning of the conversation
Of the things we see differently
The truth of what's really happening
Is somewhere lost in our arguments
We have to come to some commonality
People first, equality
Or else we'll never move forward
We have to heal this history

I STILL LOVE

I'll never hate you
For all the pain you caused
Your indifferent existence
But that was yesterday
And doesn't really matter now

I still love

Out of my life now
But I remember
Everything
How much we vibed
How we spoke the same language
    for a moment in time
And I smile

I still love

It's been years
You still come to mind
I pray you're well
And I hope life is treating you kind

Did you ever climb that mountain?
Or lasso the moon
I was convinced that you could do anything
I just believed in you

I still love
I still love, love, love…you

But more than anything, you should know
I'm sorry that I wasn't ready

I TRY

I try to make love where it does not exist
Instead of just flowing with the go
Spending time in attempts to force the emotion
Though only feeling pleasure during moments of intimacy
That's all
My heart desires to feel
But there is no edging it to be when it is not
And even looking into your eyes, I know
With certainty, it certainly is lacking
And now I am where I was
Waiting
Wanting
Longing
I'm a fiend for the euphoria
I try to tell myself lies about reality
Imagining what I wish it to be
And it's funny that I can no longer fool myself
As I once could in my youth
Laughing at the deceit I once believed
And I try to pretend not to know
This is a difficult task though
In hindsight, I gratefully fail
Yet I still try

I was just remembering

I'm remembering……
Your sweet kisses
The softness of your words whispering in my ears
Letting me know everything would be okay
Your hands gently caressing my body
The feeling of belonging
Quivering when your lips touch my neck

I'm remembering……
Intimate conversations in the dark
Your sultry eyes gazing into mine
Goodbyes with longing
Craving for time to move slowly
Wishing for things and situations that will never be
Resisting uselessly

I'm remembering……
Uncovering the kindness of your heart
The confidence of your presence
Your beautiful smile
My quiet shyness in your company
Saying no but meaning yes
Knowing everything but not caring

I'm remembering……
Wanting to call but deciding not to
T-shirts never looking so good
You pretending not to be waiting for me
Compliments that caused me to beam
Connecting without words
Being good and bad at the same time

We had fun together, didn't we?
I was just remembering

I'M HOT

Okay,
So you can see for yourself that I'm amazing
But that's not what I'm talking about
And no silly I'm not mad at you…this time
But I'm still hot
Burning up inside
Can't even get through this movie
And look-a-there
She's sitting there laughing at me
"Poor baby," my mom says, snickering
Sweating like I ran a marathon
And you know that didn't happen
Breathing like I'm in labor
Trying to fan this thing
And get my composure
CURSE YOU, hormones!
DAMN YOU, Eve!
I'm on fire
Can't even concentrate on Matt Damon
I recline in the seat
Curl up and fall asleep
Moments later I awake
But now I'm freezing
Really???
This ain't even funny!
Never wanted to be twenty something again
But right now
Sitting here in this pool of sweat and chills
Got that twenty something craziness looking GOOD
I'm hot again, DAMN!!!

I'm STILL me

Would you believe it
I'm still me
No longer a child of three
Needing
Depending
Longing to be
What I thought the older kids were
Those children all around me
Can you believe it
When I say
I'm still the me in that way
Although three score or more
I've seen many a day
Still needing
And depending
And longing to be
Until…one lonely day
I discovered, amazed
I am what I needed
Depending on me
Once that door was opened
I no longer wanted to be
Enlightened by time
You see
Only to expose
That I am,
    I am,
        I am
Still me

I'm That Woman

I'm that woman
That will love you unconditionally
But will act like you never existed
If you try and disrespect me

I'm that woman
That is fearless and free
The same woman who for ego's sake
Will feign naivety

I'm that woman
Who will have your back if you're in a bind
The same woman that will cut you loose
If I feel like you're wasting my time

I'm that woman
Who will sacrifice for our mutual gain
The same woman that laughs and jokes
But rest assured, honey, I ain't playing

I'm that woman
That tolerates you as you grow and mature
The same woman that will put you in your place
Quick, fast, and for sure

I'm that woman
That will blow your mind
The same demure, sweet, innocent acting woman
That can reign that all in, I'm well refined

I'm that woman
That calls you my one and only king
The same woman that loves, honors and cherishes you
As your beloved queen

I'm that woman
Who undoubtedly needs you
The very same woman who will go it all alone
If I have to

Don't make me have to

Intoxication

The time with you steadily slips away
This moment never to be again
But the memories are deeply rooted
I know how good the love can be

First thing in the morning...it's you
The last thought at night...you
Soooo, so, SO, so good
Is this intoxication

Though alone we're here together
Enchanting each other once more
The pleasure you give me…immeasurable
But then the noise brings me back to reality

And I don't want to stay here
Then I ask what's on your mind
You say….you…you, it's you
I believe you and long to hear you say it

And then I am back there
Yesterday, when with your touch
I surrendered everything to this
Sweet,
Sweet intoxication…

It was a woman

It was a woman
That showered me with love
When my daddy, he didn't
It was a woman
That encouraged me
When everyone said I couldn't

It was a woman
That first showed me strength
When all around me was fear
It was a woman
Whose constant guidance
Allowed me to persevere

It was a woman
That gave to me
The jewels of this world
It was a woman
That molded me
Into a woman from a girl

It was a woman
That sacrificed
So that I could succeed
It was a woman
That against all odds
Maintained our family

It was a woman
That was bold and bright
Standing all on her own
It was a woman
A single mother
That made ours a happy home

It's Over Now

You might as well get over it now
Instead of wasting years on woe
Or hoping for circumstances, improbable
Or cozying up to anger as if a dear, dear friend
Disregarding precious time, never seen again
Or recapturing the breaths in sadness lived
Or gaining just one necessary word to mend

You might as well get over it now
Your foes will have lived and died, you in despair
They're no wiser to even care
About the hurt they scattered, everywhere
And not one minute's toil delayed
Or sympathizing for their do
A stark contrasting of the two

I tell you this now, experienced
Fretting for ages gone by
Learning at his passing, I wasted time
For he had lived
And though alive, I had slowly died

I exist now, not fully comprehending
An accomplice to my own anguish for far too long
Emptiness dancing with broken pieces
Wanting a different tale, or to sing a better song
Or uselessly longing where the little girl resides
Or vainly wishing for the dead and buried, for miracles
Or for picturesque memories, so coldly denied

So be well and get over it now
Or anthems of semblance will surely sound
Or broken hearted filterings
Or regret, fully compounded

IT'S TRUE WHAT THEY SAY

It's true what they say about time
And boy how I wish I'd listened
So many things I would have done differently
So many things I would have done
Questions I would have asked
Friendships I would have mended
People I would have hugged more
Time I should have spent more wisely
Things I should have studied
Books I should have read
Beliefs I should have thrown away
Long, long ago
So many apologies
For things I've come to understand
Fear was just wasted energy
I can think of a thousand things
If I'd listened
Now time is no longer mine
And I have many regrets
My advice…
Believe what they say about time
It's true

IT'S YOU

So you say it's The Man
Causing us this pain
Tearing us down
I say that's insane
You say he is the one killing us
Robbing us blind
Turning friends to foes
With no never mind
I say you ought to look at yourself
Cause every time you fool
Elevate
Send to the top of the world
Only to take
My precious
And then you deflate
You deflate
You steal
You kill
And even worse than The Man
It's you my brother
My king
It's you that do these things to me
Just as greed
Greedy kindred sold my brothers' souls
Even today
You tear me down for your own gain
But you somehow don't see it as the same
Even worse
I say
Because I am your queen
The mother of your children
I gave you life
Only to see you take it from me
And you don't even see

That every time you use me
You abuse me
For your own gain
You, my brother
Cause me pain
So I say, it's you
Not the man
It's you that do these things

Understand?

JUST MAYBE

Just maybe when I look in your eyes
I, you awaken
I am alive
And gratitude is all that I feel
Being around you boy
For real

And just maybe
This was meant to be
Me and you
You and me
There's something we're both here to learn
Teach me baby
Don't make me yearn

Just maybe
When I met you I didn't know
How much I'd like you
That these feelings would grow
And now I'm gone
Just thinking about you
So what
What am I to do

Maybe you feel the same
This thing that started as fun
That was just a game
And now you like me too
Don't be scared baby
Just let it do what it do

And just maybe
We can change the world
The things that we do

This little black boy and girl
And once our seeds have been sown
We'll go our separate ways
Having grown

And I know that I won't forget you
And just maybe
Just maybe
You'll remember me too

JUST ONE OF THOSE DAYS

It's just one of those days
When the weight of the world is too much
When simply smiling is cumbersome
Hello
And good to see you
They don't matter
Even the laughter of children
Brings no peace
This will pass
I know for sure
So, until then
I will seek solace, quiet, stillness
It's all I know to do
Tomorrow will be better
But today is just one of those days

KISSED

I awoke
And was kissed by the sun
It held me in its arms
And we danced
Like never before
The brilliance of one little beam
Sent shivers through me
And made my entirety smile
I held on to it
Until it could no longer sustain
Waving farewell
It departed
Leaving me a gift
    – the moon
I lassoed it for myself
And danced some more
Then with a gentle kiss
I closed my eyes
Feeling only gratitude
I whispered,
Adieu

Knowing Love

Until you have been loved
The feeling of love is foreign to you
So, when asked
Responding positively
May be untrue
Unless, of course
You've been loved
A lady friend once asked me why
Smart women deal with such a guy
When knowing love's
Not what he seeks
And still she ends up in his sheets
The same reply
I do expound
Not knowing love
She fooled around
My friend
She didn't understand
Because she knew love
Again
Then
Again
So, she simply could not comprehend
Me explaining
To no avail
Cause once you know love
It does not fail
And never would you accept
Just any kind of relationship
Because you know love

Lemonade

Not a lot of history for me to remember
Didn't know much to start
This reunion of siblings, together again
Is forever etched in my mind and heart

Wonder if they realized I was looking
Soaking up their sun
Listening to stories I'd never heard before
While feasting, a patio luncheon

Watched the gathering, I was a sponge
Though, not my intention
Learning from this brief encounter
That time is a limited dimension

And then the star of the afternoon
A pitcher of sweetness, lemonade
Thinly sliced yellow slivers, my goodness
That grandpa's sister made

And there we were, in a reunion
That in a flash was done
The moment burned in memory's safe
Amazed at how fresh lemonade
    made me feel like I was home

LIGHT

Shrouded in dust
I existed
Not even knowing
One after the other they entered
Uninvited yet welcomed
Each time there was great expectation
Never stopping to evaluate their worthiness
Leaping,
Just wanting to be loved
Alone in this desire
I clung to the union's façade
If only a glimmer,
I yet embraced
Wanting…needing it to be
More enthralled by the idea than the reality
Until hope was no longer stronger
    than the truth before me
Letting go…the only choice
I reluctantly surrendered my nothing
But now there is radiance in understanding's afternoon
And I thrive in that glow
Alas…ALIVE!!!
Irrevocably illuminated

Like Oxygen

I couldn't breathe
I couldn't breathe
Suffocated by life's circumstances
And then
Out of nowhere
I was revived
Brought back to life
By the sweetness of a stranger
Not knowing my plight
But needing vitality too
Our paths crossing
With timed precision
Once again by your hands
Life was restored to my drab existence
I couldn't breathe
Each breath
Before you
Was a necessary chore
Now only gratitude
Cause you are like oxygen to me
I can breathe
I can breathe
With ease

LOOKS LIKE RAIN

Two people looking at the sky
A man and a woman
Droplets form into a choir
Splat, splat, splattering about
It's raining
One says
Can't wait for the rainbow
Says the other
The same rain
But not the same
One, reality
The other, hope
And that's the problem when looking at rain
Droplets or splashes of color
Perception is the darnedest thing

LOVED TOO

I've driven cross-country on a whim
Flown across oceans and seas
Many a wedding I did attend
Literally doing as I please

I visited The Palaces of Versailles
Even the windmills of Holland
I've given birth to many things
My imagination cannot be stunted

I've seen and greeted people galore
And spoken many tongues
Tasted cuisines from around the world
Many things I have done

I frolicked with people I cared little for
True companionship I sought
Long lasted these relationships were not
No love was even lost

I've listened to children playing
And seen their tears to boot
All these things I'd give without saying
To have loved and been loved too

maybe not

YES!!!
no???
YEs!!
nO??
Yes!
NO?
yes?
NO!
NO!!
DAMN, NOT AGAIN

more than a dream

With no more time to squander
My desire it seems was not for you
Instead, for the fantasy I created
    about us in my mind
And all the things I falsely believed we had together
It's unfortunate that it took time to realize
    that I was living in my own dream world
Where I made you the hero
And I attempted to be the damsel in distress
When in reality,
    you never wanted to be that for me
Nor did I need to be rescued
Moving on with a new perspective
Void of illusion
Hoping that the reality will one day
    be more appealing than the dream

MORNING JUXTAPOSITION

I treated myself badly
For so long
That a tender morning kiss astonished me
Simultaneously,
I was amazed and saddened
By its simplicity

my america

My America
The beautiful
And the brave
I will love you
For all of my days

Unwilling, we arrived
To build you up
On the sweat of our brow
To build you
Yet you denied
You still deny us
Equality
And opportunity
I abide
And fight to be loved
I fight to be loved!
Does that even make sense?
Knowing it is patient
Knowing it is kind
But I'm tired of waiting
For the rights
We all are guaranteed
So, I read it again
And again
Just to ensure proper interpretation
But how can I misconstrue
All persons born…
Have equal protection of the laws?
I have my birth certificate right here
And it's says USA
Something ain't right!
No wonder we're broken
I'm broken

And bitter
No wonder
But I still love you
My America
And I wonder if I'm right to
When you don't see me
You don't see me my mocha
As amazing
And my brothers
You slaughter at will
Where's the equal protection in that?
How do we tell our children of your greatness?
Cause, you are great!
Juxtaposed with warnings of your danger
And we have to tell them
For their survival
HOW IS THIS STILL HAPPENING?
How?
And I am repeatedly saddened
Cause I love my America
Even though you never loved me
You never loved us
You are not alone in this culpability
I am your assistant
Disenfranchising myself voluntarily
Lacking available knowledge
Failing to share with my brothers and sisters
Hiding the ladder
Instead of holding it
Valuing rims, and Tims and gems and Kim
No, no, no, no
NO!
We are a collective
And none of that stuff matters
Not really

And you can't even comprehend
When we say
Our Lives Matter!
Cause you'll never have to walk in these shoes
Not even an effort to understand
Screaming, 'all lives matter',
And, 'get over it'
Just how do you propose we do that,
My America?
When these things are still happening
EVERY
SINGLE
DAY
In my America
The only solution I see
Is excellence
So, we'll be excellent
And despite what I see
What you see
Know that there was a dream
Of a King
That lives
And is still possible
In my America

MY BEAUTIFUL SURRENDER

One day I was riding down a two-lane country road
Out there all alone
Me and the open air
Trees framed the way as I passed on by
Each one its own greeting
The sky was a crystal blue
Breezy out, but only subtle breaths
Window down, a musical serenade
And I just let it all go right on out the window
I let go of everything that I was clinging to
All the memories that no longer served me
The people who said they loved me but really didn't
Of old thought patterns and behaviors
And all the false stories
I told myself about myself
    over
        and over
            and over again
None of it even bothered a goodbye
Nor endeavored to stay behind
So, I left everything right out there on that country road
It was no longer mine
Never had been really
Just comfortable and familiar
So, I drove…
    and I drove…
        and I drove some more…
I drove right smack dab into my surrender
And that was absolutely all mine
And it is beautiful

MY MYSTERY

I was a young woman when I knew
That I could get a man with my
Ooooohhh…

So for many years
I must confide
I gave away my golden prize

And men
They loved it
Oh yes, they do
But in the end
Alone again
Not one stayed true

It took me time to realize
I am more than what's between my thighs
And I can't blame men like you
Who are taking time to realize this too

So, when I am passing you by
My smile
My curves
They catch your eyes
Your first thought shouldn't be
How can I get inside that lady?

Because I am more than just a hole
I am a Queen
If truth be told
And it's sad that when you look at me
A hole is all you see

So, don't approach me with yo silly lines

Hey girl,
Here's my number
Call me some time

Cause you can't be with me
When...
You have a wife
Or a friend

Not arrogant
Nor am I proud
But I am going to tell you
And I'll say it real loud
If a hole is all you see
You'll never know my mystery

my tears are my strength

You hurt me deeply
I say this without hesitation
And yes, I am emotional
But my tears
In no way compromise my strength
In fact,
When I am vulnerable
I am my most powerful
For it is in my vulnerability
That I trust in love the most
And although I tell you I love you
That you are missed
I am secure in the knowledge
That no matter which way you run
I will be all right
So, I will continue to love without fear
Without regret
And sometimes I may get hurt
But with each tear a lesson is learned
So, I welcome every opportunity to love
Every lesson
Every tear
Because my tears are my strength
They don't compromise me
They never have

new me

Was afraid of you
You were someone new to see
Said yes, I knew me

no instructions necessary

Wouldn't it be nice
If life came with a how-to manual?
Though even with instructions
It can all go so, so wrong
The good thing,
Most mistakes can be fixed
With just a little tweaking,
Or a simply stated apology

no more

No more (matter of fact)
No more (emphatic)
No more (sad)
No more (mad)
No more (hurt)
No more (crying)
No more (defiant)
No more (laughing)
No more (guaranteed)

no more rose

You are back
But still the same
The rose, however, is gone
Not needing or longing for what used to be
Just remembering wonderful feelings
I listen to you,
Unmoved by the lyrics that once controlled me
And I laugh,
While you misinterpret reminiscing
    as desire to be again
I'll wage my heart on another
Because I've already read your story
And I'm not at all interested in the sequel
So, I smile at your attempts
But no questions remain
Silence authors my response
Silly boy,
You had your chance

No Regrets

The man that wants me
Can't wait to see
The beauty that I possess
What I need from a man
I'm quite sure you understand
Is much more than what I can get when we undress

I am grateful for the times we had
It wasn't all bad
I loved the way you made me smile
So, with no regrets
Me, boy you won't forget
You helped take my mind off my troubles for a while

But I know
It's time for me to go
I guess this is the beginning of a new season
Now while we're still friends
This thing has to end
Because you broke my heart for no reason

I must say that I will miss
Your sweet kiss
And the way you held my hand
And oh, your beautiful smile
That drives me so wild
That's why there are no regrets, my friend

not enough

Today I know what I want
For today
For tomorrow
For forever
Tomorrow what I want may change
But today I know
With certainty
That it does not look like this
I never raised my hand
Or asked
If this was okay
No excuses now though
I know
Today I know
So, I choose to ascend
This present situation
As is
Good is not good enough
A little better doesn't mean all right
What you're offering
It's not enough
And I refuse to beg for ordinary
Ever again

not now

Don't give up now
In the midst of this storm
What do you mean you can't make it
Don't you know who you are

And no, it ain't gon' be easy
But you already knew
So get up! Get up, keep going
No choice but to make it through

No weapon can stop you
Don't you know your Source
You can accomplish whatever you tell yourself
May as well stay the course

Because even in this darkness
Know that the light still shines
Just look, there's the moon, there're the stars
Radiantly glowing in the sky

Though you may fail repeatedly
With each lesson, you cannot lose
So don't you dare give up, not now
The perspective is up to you

OFFERINGS

He hadn't a thing
    but kindness to offer me
And I welcomed him with open arms
Wanting it to be enough
Although I already knew it wouldn't be
Not this time
If only we had met
    long, long ago
When kindness
    was my only offering

OH, WRETCHED BITTERNESS

I was angry
I knew it wasn't me
But it was…
It was the me that didn't give all I had
That didn't commit enough to being, just a little better
The me that watched
As all my friends lived
I, only existing
There were other reasons too
Things beyond my control
Pushing me to be bitter
Societal things
    …sexism
        …racism
All the 'isms' you can imagine
At some point, I tolerated them
Naïve and afraid
And now here I am
Wedged in this bitterness
Between I don't care no more
And craving to be different
Wanting love without ulterior motives
And respect, just because
I'm hoping these simple desires aren't too much to ask for
Cause this is exhausting
My shoulders are hunched
from the heaviness that accompanies it
It sure would be nice to be free
My hands are raised in surrender, focusing on love
Praying it's enough to break the chains of bitterness

on exercise

I loathe working out
But after I exercise
I feel AMAZING!

on getting naked

long ago
I stopped getting naked…
circumstances
of which I had no control
a little girl
just blooming
I stopped…
I know what can happen
not desiring that
I don't
I won't get naked!
feeling dirty
and forever stained
unable to comprehend
these feelings
all I know…
don't get naked!
so, I hide.
now, all grown
behind the clothes
and the feelings,
the skin and the sadness
even now…
knowing why
I still don't get naked

On Pebbles

Thank You
Yesterday is gone
Just a pebble
Vainly attempting to distract me
From the magnificence that awaits
In my eternity

Pebbles and Stones

A pebble cast in the ocean
Creates ripples that spawn into eternity
That's what a pebble will do
Carelessly he threw stones
Birthing infinite waves
And repercussions

POPCORN CEILINGS

We were talking
About nothing good
Tears streaming from all involved
She lay on her back
I'm holding her hands
Hoping to prevent the hits that I deserve
And out of nowhere
She says, "I HATE POPCORN CEILINGS!"
Immediately I look at her
My eyes following hers
And I understood
"When I get a house,
I'll have no popcorn ceilings."
As if a house without popcorn ceilings
    will be the solutions for our problems
And I nod
Although a bit confused, I agree
And that was the end of it
No more tears
Not even another mention of the previous topic
We lay beside one another, silent
Looking up at the popcorn ceilings
I'm thinking, how can I fix this?
And she, I'm sure, is planning her out
And in no time at all, we drifted

POSSIBLe

Is it possible that we were both
    doing the best that we knew how to do?
And somewhere in that doing
We simply didn't know how to give to the other
    the thing most needed
Wanting but failing over and over again
When hearts long for love,
    why is the path so hard?
Especially, when there are two, equally eager
Why can't we feel the truth of what the other is giving
And release our messed-up expectations
Expectations of how and what it should be like
Oh, how I desire a pure heart
Wishing to erase the clouds cast by past pains
Unfairly comparing hiStory to tainted memories
That obviously I have yet to let go
And that's not fair to either of us
In tears, I apologize incessantly to myself and to you
Hoping the vibrations of my truth will be conveyed
Weariness defeats my crying
I surrender to sleep's restoration
Love, my first and last contemplation
Hope, a forever companion
A faint smile surfaces
Knowing with certainty,
I'll see love again

Precious Peace

The unfortunate thing about men
    is that if you decide to take them back after a betrayal
If they haven't learned or matured
They'll think that you'll get over it again
    the next time
        and the time after that
Each 'THIS IS IT!' declaration carries less weight
In fact, you'll start to even doubt it yourself
Every time chipping away at your esteem
With words of self-loathing
Instead of thinking of ways to make the relationship better
They use their energy
Coming up with craftier ways of deception
So, it's really up to you
And if you're willing to take that chance…again
Decide!
Because alone doesn't mean lonely,
    unless you allow it to
And nothing in the world is more precious than your peace

The Road

When you're faced with wrong or right
Which road will you choose?
When your love done gone
Made you a fool
And the pain is impossible to bare
When all you remember is the sweet embrace
No memory of their callousness
Which road will you choose?
When you gave all you knew how to give
At every opportunity you did
When with a loving heart
No care did they give
Which road will you choose?
Each moment now you struggle
Decision already made
Love unreciprocated

Role Model

I'm not your role model
I did it all the wrong way
Not listening to the truth
When it was before me
Running from challenges
Instead of facing them head on
Looking for love
In all the wrong places
No, I'm not a role model
Although I may look the part
Dressed to conceal
I'm not who or where I want to be
But I'm not complaining about it
I had all the opportunities
    right in the palm of my hands
I still do
Yet I watch
As peers who were afforded less surpass me
In all the ways that count
I'm full of regret
I hope you're paying attention
I'm not the role model
Though not a sad anthem
Just my declaration
Long in the making
A cry for time
For me to sort my life out
Though I'm starting to believe
I should just jump in headfirst,
Not worrying if it'll go right or wrong
Doing it better this time
More conscious, more aware
Here I go

same ole me with you

It's been some time now
Since me and you
One day turning into the next
Memories fading into forgetfulness
Never crossing my mind, really
And then one day
We come face to face again
And as we talk about things
Old and new
I melt into that little girl
The one I was with you, giggly and shy
Realizing that we've both moved on
Neither one of us desiring the other
Yet still admiring those things
    that once bound us together
And as we depart again
I'm forced to admit
    that I'm still the same ole me with you
Familiar and uncomfortable
The woman that I've become
    struggles to recognize that girl
Haven't seen that me since you
I thought she was gone forever
And finally, after all this time
I'm glad that we parted

Seasons Are Changing

Driving down the same old roads
It seems as though things have changed
When I was here before
    the trees were full of green leaves
Now, the colors of autumn illuminate the beautiful blue sky
And for the first-time
    my eyes notice the magnificence of crimson
I'm seeing the brilliance of gold,
    the splendor of tangerine
And then the wind blows
A myriad of colors glide aimlessly everywhere
And at that very moment jealously overtakes me
I long for the freedom of autumn leaves
Destination unknown but flowing anyway
I believe the leaves, they know
Tomorrow they will have another opportunity to fly
And with the season's change they will reemerge
So, they just let go
But for me I continue to cling tightly to yesterday
Wishing for the colors of days gone by
Afraid of what the change in season will bring
I liken myself to the evergreen
But when I close my eyes,
I imagine that I am an autumn leaf
Floating with the breeze
Dancing without purpose
But oh, there is a purpose to the rhythm,
    to the dance
The leaves, they know
That's why they are able to let go

Then I see myself floating
Gliding with the wind
And realize my eyes are wide open

And I am driving
Although down the same old roads
It seems as though,
I am changing

THE SHIRT

Hanging in the closet
That red shirt you used to wear
Your favorite
When I see it,
I am instantly taken back
To the last time I recall you wearing it
A smile comes across my face
Simultaneously,
I wrestle to hold back tears
I'm thinking of you, of us
In the same breath
Almost as if I were reaching out to grab your hand
I take hold of one sleeve
And place it against my cheek
Trying to feel you one last time
I close my eyes
And your scent
Ever so faint
Fills me as I inhale
And without control
I grab the shirt as if you were standing there
Wearing it
Desperately attempting to remember
What it felt like to hold you in my arms
Without even realizing
I lose my balance
And fall against the closet door
Longing, aching,
For you to be here with me once again
Wearing your shirt

sometimes

He hasn't a thing
But kindness to offer me
Sometimes that's enough

spilled milk

I have wasted time
That I can never get back
On meaningless things

SOUL MEET

I've waited my soul life to meet you,
    and you,
        and you,
           and you
Each one of you
A precisely timed encounter
Here to show me something about myself
    that I have forgotten
And to reveal what I needed
A necessity for my next journey
Our souls have been trying to unite
Crossing paths on numerous occasions
Without even knowing that we were destined to be
What lessons have you come to teach me
I welcome all the possibilities
    and am anxious to know you
So, before you become the love of my life
Before I call you friend
Before crying at your funeral
Before thinking that I hate you
Before our time together is over
Before our paths diverge and I never see you again
I want to thank you now
Because of you,
    and you,
        and you,
           all of you
I am different
In ways that I never imagined before you
And all these miracles happened to me, to us
Because our souls agreed to meet

STILL

Chills you bring me
Still today
Just seeing you walk
And uummm…..
The way you say my name
It brings these same feelings in me
Still I love these things, you see
To look in your eyes
Every time a surprise
Can't believe
You still have a hold
You're beautiful to behold
And I'm wishing
Of things to be
But just seeing you
Still, is enough for me

STILL SOUL DREAMIN'

Who could I be,
    if I loved me some me?

SUBSTANTIATED CRY

Yesterday I cried
Although I already knew
Substantiated

The Sun Will Shine Again

One day I had a date on the porch
I was looking for answers
A bird soared toward the sky
And it told me that I should fly

Curiously looking to the clouds
They responded in kind
They told me
Watch how we move
How we float
How we glide
And on occasion the sun
It will hide
But you should know
It will always shine

And then the trees
They blew in the breeze
Spoke of renewal
And of ease

For hours I sat and listened
And watched
The sun sashayed over the hill
Uniquely waving goodbye
Just before it sighed
It's time for me to go

I was reminded
By the murmurs of crimson and gold
Even when the sun is gone
I can recall its beauty
All around
In everything

And just like that
It was gone
Whispering in retreat
I'll see you again
And tomorrow, I will be reborn

sweet betrayals

Time has taught me well
That actions tell the stories
Your sweet words betray

sweet sax

your sound had me misconstrued
so much so that I saw you standing at the end of the aisle
waiting on me to say I do
I do love your melodies
vibrating in my ears
making love to me so sweetly
swaying to feelings you evoked in me
I am adrift
staring at the loveliness of the summer sky
sitting on the beach under an umbrella with you
holding hands with your music
the drums beating to the rhythm of my heart
the bass playing my body into motions
I hadn't made since…
well…last night
you continuously stroked me
with those crescendos and vibratos
causing me to forget any yesterday
I was in the moment with you
loving every note you whispered in my ear
the passion I felt crept right up and kissed my neck
causing me to shiver in anticipation of your next note
every molecule in my body danced
thoroughly satisfied
I couldn't control anything anymore
and when the serenade ended
I exhaled
aching for more of that sweet sax
for more of the Marcus Anderson experience

THERE, THEIR, THEY'RE

There up on the hilltop
Their faces red in the sun
They're ready to go
3   2   1
The race has just begun

THINK IT THROUGH

Sometimes you just have to take a DEEP breath...
Before you choke the life out of someone,
Lose your job,
'Cause you're the defendant in a murder trial
Now you have no money
Convicted twenty to life
Can't vote
Or binge watch *House of Cards* on a Wednesday night
Can't eat scallops for lunch at your favorite Japanese joint
Or sit on the toilet
    after you've finished doing what you do
    looking around at all the places you need to scrub
Oh, or write long silly messages
Who could give all this up?
Think I'll just take a DEEP breath...
    and carry myself to sleep

THINKIN'

He ain't thinkin' bout me
At least
Not like that
He just be doin' thangs
Thangs that feel like he be
Thinkin' bout me
But no, he not
I think bout him like that
Like I wanna be all in love
Kissin and cuddlin'
Like I wanna be his
And he be mine
That's how I'm thinkin' bout him
But he ain't thinkin' bout me
Even though my phone ring
All the time
Talkin' all night bout
Relevant and irrelevant
When I goes away
He say he miss me
And it make me all warm inside
Make me think I'm all on his mind
That he thinkin' bout me
Like that
But he ain't
That's what he say
And I be all confused
Not understandin' why
Why if he be callin'
And he be missin'
Why it ain't like that
But it not
That's what he say
And that's what I gotta believe

Not what I see
But what he say
Jus gotta stop thinkin'
Bout him
I guess

Time Has a Way

It's easy to forget exactly how things used to be
Time has a way of clouding old memories
I recall the days when I could smell your presence
When you were nowhere around
I would catch your scent in old clothes
And immediately be transported to that time and place
But time has its way
And I can't recall those things anymore
I don't even remember what fragrance you wore
There was a time when your words
    would continuously sing in my ears
And without any reason, I would smile
Used to be your touch would last until I touched you again
But time has a way of casting shadows
And as days turn into months
There's a tendency to forget the little things
    that only breaths ago could not be ignored
I cried when we parted
I didn't want it to be over, but it was
I can still remember the way you would kiss my hand
    when we talked
I used to be able to remember the feeling of your lips
    against my skin
But time has a way of blurring those thoughts
And although I try,
I can't bring myself to conjure those thoughts
    or feelings anymore
I think your soft kisses are what got me
But who knows for sure now?
There are so many things that come to mind when I think
    about you and me
But the details of any particular event have faded
Who needs details anyway when they no longer matter?
Forgetting the things that I used to love,

    saddens me sometimes
At the same time, I'm grateful
Grateful for love
For loss
For great friends
For new beginnings and endings
For healing
But most of all,
I am grateful for time

TODay

today
this very minute
I will stop trying to figure out
if this is love
whatever it is, it is
I will allow myself
to feel
whatever
it is
I will cry
I will pray
I will grow
and then
one day this pain
will subside
I know this to be true
I anticipate that day
that moment
anxiously
until then
I will
just be
still
so that the next time
you or this situation
presents itself to me
I will remember
and I will pay attention
so that this lesson
will never have to be taught
again

TOUCH UP PAINT

Everything that made me think about you
I just erased with a touch of paint
Surprised at how easy it was to delete you
Wondering why it took me so long to say goodbye
Regardless,
It's done

United, We'll Stand!

We were emancipated in 1865
With that proclamation
That's what they teach us
But we're still slaves
In many, many, many ways
And that Jim Crow
They said he was dead
But he's alive and breathing
Right here in my neighborhood
Hiding behind the 13th
And public lynchings
They're still public
Although they'll try and convince us
That it doesn't happen no more
But I saw it with my own eyes
Last week and the week before that
    and the week before that one
And one and one and one more
Too many sons dying
They're lying
Lying dead in the streets
Emmett don't even have to be accused of
    whistling no more
And we're still marching
Like my mama and my mama's mama
And her mama too
Way before I was born
Not even hiding behind sheets no more
They're right there on tv
Campaigning to lead us
Further behind
And our choice
Is not to voice our opinions
Not to vote

Oh, righteous indignation
After the boycotts of Parks,
And the marching,
And all that dying
And killing of the King
How dare you
Foolish, foolish sun
We'll rise again, Maya
No more play, play, playing pretend
Did I hear that it's not your struggle?
Mr. and Ms. white privilege
If it doesn't affect you
Why should you care
Mr. young, black and rich millionaire
Don't you feel that knife in your back?
That rope around your neck
Tightening.
It's tightening.
But you're not your brother's keeper
Didn't you know
You are your brother
Do the right thing
Wake up
We're not yet free
And that's why they're taking a knee
Raising fists in solidarity
And screaming WE MATTER!
It's got to get mo' better
These blues
Some of us don't get the clues
Can't you see those lyrics you're singing
That's what's bringing pain
Stop contributing to this reign
And sing with me
You are beautiful, you are smart, you are special
Won't you help

So, our children won't believe
Those alternative facts
Instead they'll know the truth
In their hearts
And in their minds
I know it can be done
If only we could stand,
United as one

VIOLIN

I never wanted to play the violin
Especially not for you
But I became an unintentional virtuoso,
A reluctant prodigy
Due to years of betrayal,
Years of neglect
They call me Ms. Chang
But Sarah is my name
Or even Marcus
That Wil B. just fine too
I laugh at the repeated, 'I really miss you's'
And the 'I love you's'
Can't you see that I don't even hear you
That I don't really care…not anymore
Don't you hear my violin playing, fool
My invisible bow strumming back and forth,
Back and forth
A concerto in B sharp,
Just for you

Ha, ha, ha, ha, ha
Ahhhh!

wait a minute

You don't understand,
When you say you have to go
And I say,
Noooooooooooo…
Hold on, wait a minute.
Just one more thing
You see me as trying to be controlling
And that's not it at all
I just want one more second
One more smile, one more touch
Just one more
Whatever with you
That's all
Just one more
To take me
Until the next moment with you
I don't know why I am this way
Sometimes it feels as though
I'll never see your face again
Sometimes
It's just entirely too long between this time
And the next
And sometimes
I am simply trying to memorize you
With my eyes
With all my senses really
So that I can endure this separation
And at that moment
When you want to go
I haven't quite taken you all in
And I just need time to stand still
So please…
Wait, just one more minute

WAIT TO FREE

Caged men are choice-less
We'll wait until you are free
Then I'll see, still me?

WHAT I LIKE

I like the breeze
When outside its seventy degrees
And above a beautiful blue
Clouds in the sky
The sun peeping through
I like sandy beaches
In the fall
And juicy peaches
Not mushy at all
I like great books
That captivate me
And children playing
This, I love to see
I like competition
Although you wouldn't know
But being the best
Just motivates me so
I like music
And songs
That cause my soul to dance
I like your sweet kisses
Your melody
Holding your hand
And at the end of the night
Not too cool
Temperature just right
When asleep
I like to dream
And when morning breaks
Opportunity to do what I like once again

WHAT IS THIS

If it's not love,
Then why am I feeling so,
    so, so, so hurt
Sometimes I want to play the game
And sometimes I can't
I simply can't
What is it
I feel so many things that I haven't felt before
So many wonderful things
My mind is so stimulated
All of my senses have been awakened
Then there are the things
The bad things that I have felt over and over again
The things and feelings
    that I never want to experience again
What do I do?
I miss the sweet words that were once
    uttered from those juicy lips
I miss the soft kisses
I miss the phone calls any time of the day
I keep telling myself you want me
But if that was so,
I would know

WHAT TO DO

I remember sitting on the floor
Our legs intertwined
Staring into each other's eyes
I begin to cry
Although I feel so at home with you
I've been here before
Fear overcomes me
Memories of pain surround our caress
At that moment, you grab me tight
You ask, 'what's wrong'
Looking into your eyes
I see sincerity
And I feel as though I can trust you, with me
'I don't want to hurt again,' I say
We continue our embrace
Softly
You whisper in my ear
A promise
I'll never hurt you
This I haven't heard before
I felt your words
And I believe
But as I sit here today
Missing us
I cry
Because you kept your promise
Now, what do I do

When You Know

Why do you fall
When you know what you know
Why do you let your heart go
Why do you give
Without condition
When conditionally you're given
And left crying you wonder
When you know what you know
Will there ever be a time
When love is returned
In the manner that you express
Or forever you're to ask
For love's caress
And without fear
You'll fall once again
When you know what you know
To be fictitious
Why do you fall
When you know what you know

WHERE WE LEFT IT

First comes the connection
Divinely orchestrated just for two
Then the world generously provides opportunities
For you both to learn from one another
Through shared experiences and carefree interactions

Sometimes you just won't see eye to eye
But over time, you both will change
In ways you never imagined
And without even knowing it
The friendship claims a piece of your soul as its own

Forever

Regardless of whatever else happens
You'll always remember with fondness
The silly laughter, the tearful late-night phone calls,
The bond that can't be replaced by anything or anyone

And when you see each other again
All the things that wedged themselves between you
    – the years, the family, the career, the distance
They instantly disappear

And everything is as it once was
Where you left it
When life interfered

WHY I SHINE

When the weight of the world is upon me
And I need a light to shine
I look all around me
And I claim, 'This is all mine'
From the leaves that swing in the trees
To the petals of lavender and gold
They were created to be appreciated
And their opulence restoreth my soul
There, little creatures
Scurrying all about
All these things are blessings
For me to see and shout
I will shine
I will shine
I do shine
At Your grace
And I am restored
For the world to see

WISH

If there were a wish
It would be for us to see
Life the way it used to be
You and I together
Remembering then
You and I making plans
Parting
Thought it would never
Be this way
The way we are today
Seldom do we see one another
I wish for life to rewind
Back to more
Intimate times
When we were lovers of life
And many other things
We were truly friends
I miss that
Way back when
If I had a wish
My wish would be
For you and me
To be like it used to be,
    before…

WITHIN

This is not a race to be won
Although there is a definite end
Hopefully before that point is reached
You find the peace within

woman

A woman that knows her worth
Is the most powerful creature
On the face of the earth

woman power

Heart broke, you picked her
Wasted too much time with you
Now, I wonder why

YOU ARE

You are breath
Necessary and easy
You are a smile
In a concert of frowns
A distraction
Pure satisfaction
You are calm
In a storm
A break from the norm
You are motivation
Stimulation
Moving me to explore
More and more
And MORE
You are staccatos
And vibratos
Inspiring song
You are good mornings
And GOOD nights
You make it all right
To just be me
You are a chocolate surprise
A sensational rise
Whenever I am with you
You are coy
Not liking that much
But boy…it makes you, you
You are a familiar mystery
The lock, and the key
And all I need you to be,
You are

YOUR WORST enemy

Though you'd like to blame someone else
To point the finger too
It would certainly be much easier
But something you simply can't do

You'd like to say it's all their fault
To cloak them with this shame
Even though no evidence
Can tie it to their name

There're reasons why you're stuck right now
Treading hopelessly astray
Still yourself temporarily
With this you'll find a way

Take a moment to contemplate
Although a difficult pursuit
And stop accusing everyone else
Your own worst enemy is you

GET NAKED WITH ME

THE BREAKDOWN...

ACCOMPLICE - p. 1

I have never seen America as divided as it is now, though I am certain that this discord has always existed, gauging our tempestuous history. There were times of far worse injustice and struggle than that which is currently taking place, including but not limited to slavery, Jim Crow, the civil rights movement, women's suffrage, and LGBT inequality.

I may have been asleep or simply never personally seen prejudice so blatantly flaunted. The advent of social media makes these cowardly acts appear more prevalent. I don't want to give a voice to anyone by naming names. But what I know to be true is that no one person can suppress another person or group alone. Many must agree and comply for such malice to persist and be sustained.

The fact that intelligent people, some that I have at one point in my life called friend, collude to do and/or say nothing about the egregious behavior of the current 'leaders' is intolerable. These atrocious acts are so disheartening and frankly downright scary, requiring people of conscience to stand up and act, and to call a spade a spade.

To be clear, there is no amount of money, or judicial nominations, or tax cuts, or lack of an adequate immigration policy that warrants the acceptance of the ignorance, injustice, and depravity that has occurred as of late by people in leadership roles.

What are we teaching our children? What are we teaching the world?

These feelings are what birthed this poem that I wrote many years ago. And with each passing day, the words of this prose ring louder and truer than ever before. Yet, I still hold out hope for this country to become the America that I believed her to be when I was a child.

AIN'T NOBODY GON KNOW – p. 2
Change is challenging!

Let's just start there. And for the kicker, the longer you wait to do what you're going to have to do anyway to get where you want to be, the more challenging it is.

I loathe exercising! But exercise loves me.

One day I was going over different options in my head of how I could get out of working out, how to trick my Peloton into saying I had ridden it, when I really hadn't. I had set a goal to exercise 90 days straight and really didn't feel like getting on that bike that day. Mind you, two-thirds of this goal had already been accomplished, so I was on the downside, as I like to say when I have completed more than half of any task.

Just as soon as those plots to self-sabotage came, I was instantly flooded with thoughts of nobody would know, much less care if I didn't ride that bike. The only person who would know and who it would matter to would be me. And in that moment, I realized that sabotaging myself again, was not on the table that day.

From these never-ending negotiations to treat myself better, this poem was born. Another 'change is challenging' type poem is *On Exercise* - p. 97.

ANCHORED - p. 4

Since my divorce I have been in a constant state of dating. Sadly, this has been going on for years. The only consistent theme in all of my encounters is that no one, including myself, was perfect. Each of us searching to be loved despite our limitations.

There was one relationship in particular that spawned this poem and a few others in this book including *Hope Possibly* - p. 53, *Offerings* - p. 95, *Possible* - p. 101 and *Sometimes* - p. 109.

The man in question was lighter skinned than I had been accustomed to, which is only useful to illuminate my past preference. He wasn't muscular, at all. In fact, you could tell he used to be heavy at one time, which would have been fine with me. What drew me to him more than anything else was his smile. His smile was electric.

For the first time in my life I remember being able to see this man. I mean, really see him. Not with my eyes. With my heart. He wanted to be loved just like I did. If only love were enough to sustain anything. And the fact that neither one of us had our shit together didn't help at all. He was a divorced father of two and was always working.

He had a full-time job and a side hustle. That working all the time should have been a red flag, but he was so damn refreshing, a man that was reliable, who wanted to be in a relationship, and kissed me like I was the most beautiful creature on the face of the earth. And besides, he liked me in all my mess, and I needed to be liked.

At the time I was separated and had been for over ten years. And I wanted/needed to be rescued and he seemed to be ripe for the challenge. The rub was that he needed rescuing too, and I had been rescuing men in one way or another all my adult life, long before he ever entered the picture. I simply didn't have the energy to save one more man.

The second red flag was that I felt lonely a lot while in this relationship. Loneliness is an awful feeling when you're involved with someone. What made it worse is that I had spent much of my adult life single and I had never felt lonely before, ever. So of course, this feeling was really shocking and unwelcomed.

I had so much hope for us. God knows I wanted to love him, but there just was no forcing it. After the initial 'giddy, he likes me' was over, I couldn't see past all the things he was that were incompatible with who I was, all the things he didn't have, nor wanted, that I desired in a mate.

Looking back on it now, I wish I had been woman enough to love him, because he was a damn good man. He just wasn't the right good man for me.

ANOTHER MINUTE - p. 5

When I first started writing this poem I was thinking about my relationship with my father, or lack thereof. He had recently passed away, and the experience I had with him and my extended family during his last days was both devastating and exuberant.

My father was one of fourteen kids. Needless to say, I have a big family, most of whom I've never met, including some uncles and many, many cousins. I knew my five aunts but hadn't seen them all together, in one place, ever before this.

Deaths are melancholy family reunions, where you are glad to see and meet people you haven't seen or spoken to in decades, but sad at the same time for the occasion at hand. I met cousins I didn't know, made new friends over spades and storytelling, all of us connecting in this inevitable farewell. Collectively we all vowed to stay in touch, to vacation together. Sincere words spoken in vain.

I was like a sponge soaking up all the stories I never knew. One particular cousin meticulously told story after story of how my father was like a father to her, rescuing her from herself when she was a child. I was jealous, not having fond stories of my own to recount. She clearly loved my father, even referred to him by his nickname. Her father was my father's uncle and best friend, though they were the same age.

Friends of his, some I knew, some I didn't, visited and added to the stew of tales I was absorbing. Sad but true, I got to know my father more during the last week of his life than I ever had. He had lived and he was loved, and he loved me and my brother in the best way he knew how. That's what I came to understand from all of this.

This poem sums up my feeling about that brief time, the last time with my father and all my family and friends. And the more I read it, the more I reminisce about all the love ones that have gone on, and how I'd give anything to have just one more moment with them.

Some other poems inspired by my father include *Baby Girl* - p. 6, *Daddy Should Have* - p. 22, *I Believed You* - p. 55, *It's Over Now* - p. 67 and *Pebbles and Stones* - p. 99.

BREATHLESS GLORY - p.11

Not much to say about this one really, only that I was feeling total exhilaration when I wrote it.

My family and I had gone on a 3-day Disney Dream Cruise to the Bahamas. I wrote this on the last evening after leaving their amazing private island. That day my mom and I had paddle boated across the clear blue water, picnicked on the beach, and rented a bike with some friends, touring the island, before heading back to our suite.

Sitting on the veranda taking in the view as we set sail on the way back to Cape Canaveral, I was in awe, not wanting to leave or get ready for dinner. My mom beckoned for me to hurry up, again and again. I resisted with my entire soul until the day yielded to the night.

If you've ever felt bliss like I felt out on the balcony that night, you'll never forget it as long as you live. Its been six years since then and the memory still lingers like the pungent smell of hydrangeas.

Nature evokes these feelings in me all the time, forcing me to put pen to paper. Poems with similar themes and inspiration include *The Chirper's Revival* - p. 14, *From the Front Porch* - p. 38, *Good Morning Sunshine* - p. 45 and *Home in Autumn* - p. 51.

CRYING, FOR ALL OF YOU - p. 19

It doesn't come as a surprise that black men and women are being unjustly slaughtered in America. It should. But it is as American as apple pie and baseball. For a 2-month period in 2016, blacks were being killed by or dying in the custody of police, back to back. It was maddening. One of the most egregious murders was that of Philando Castile. Philando's girlfriend had the where-with-all to record the entire incident. After I watched the video and saw the little girl in the backseat, I was even more infuriated and devastated. How is this still going on? As more and more of these murders happen and are exposed by video, I am reminded that many times we would be in the dark about these heinous murders if not for the footage.

I wonder how our ancestors made it. They were even more oppressed. I think I would have gone mad living during slavery, or Jim Crow, or the Civil Rights movement. Each time I hear of another murder, a tiny piece of my soul dies. James Baldwin's quote, "To be a negro in this country and to be relatively conscious, is to be in a rage almost all of the time. So that the first problem is how to control that rage so that it won't destroy you," sums up exactly how I feel, on a regular basis.

This poem is a tribute to all the black men and women who have been unjustly murdered.

My America - p. 83 and *United, Well Stand!* - p. 122, are poems that reverberate my feelings about the injustice and inequities happening in America, still.

As I was finalizing this book, at least three more black lives were snuffed out by cops and white supremacists. I'm crying for you Ahmaud Arbery. I'm crying for you Breonna Taylor. I'm crying for you George Floyd. I'm crying for you Rayshard Brooks. I'm crying for all of you!

EN GARDE – *p. 30*

The lesson from this poem is to *follow your intuition*. The basic question posed is: Are you going to act on the longings of your heart, or are you going to make the wisest decision based on the information available to you at the time?

Many times, I have known everything I needed to know to make an informed decision, but because I wanted what I wanted (chocolate cake, a man, sex) I didn't make the wise choice. The ironic thing about doing this is that eventually things will get so bad, you get tired of dealing with the bs, or the other person will force your hand and you'll end up where you should have been in the first place, with a few unnecessary detours, having gone through hell and high water to get there, when you didn't have to.

P was his nickname. We had briefly entertained a relationship in high school. But then I got back with the guy I loved before heading off to college. Thirty years later he pops up as a friend suggestion on Facebook. He had always been a handsome dude but handsome is not a reason to date someone, let them move in with you, or fall in love.

I'd heard through the grapevine that he had been asking about me, for years. So, when I saw the Facebook profile, I clicked on it to be nosy. He had buffed up a lot and eventually I found out why. He was separated and so was I, and thought, 'why not.' Since we lived in different cities we communicated via cell and facetime.

His stint in prison limited his employment opportunities but he was working, in construction. After three weeks of talking every night and a lot of phone sex he said he was ready – ready to get back together, ready to move to where I was, ready to move in with me. I saw a million red flags flashing in neon. To make a long story short, I wasn't ready for any of that. I knew him, but I didn't know him well enough for all of that. And the idea of having some man that I really didn't know move in my house scared the shit out of me. So, I ghosted him.

En Garde is the story of my internal struggle, wanting to be in a relationship, wanting to make love, yet knowing I didn't want to take on everything that he was, or had been through. Besides the fact that he was still very married. And I've learned the hard way that separated is married.

ENDINGS - p. 31

I know this is none of y'all, but sometimes in the name of love we put up with mess we should absolutely never accept. When in fact, love looks the exact opposite.

I want to say, a person that loves you won't cheat on, hit, disrespect, or demean you. But I'm not sure if that's true, at all. And some understandably would disagree with me. But I can make this assessment because I have loved, I mean, truly loved friends, family and partners and have said and done some awful things to them.

What I can say with certainty, is that a person who loves you should not do these things. But what I am more certain of is that you shouldn't allow people the treat you poorly.

Nina Simone famously said, "You've got to learn to leave the table when love is no longer being served." This mantra is the gist of *Endings;* learning to love yourself enough to walk away when you're not getting what you need or deserve. Leaving someone that you have invested your heart in is a badass boss move, that is only possible if you truly love yourself.

Fair Warnings - p. 34, piggybacks off this theme of loving yourself. It took me a while to get here, but I live in this drama free space now.

FROM THE FRONT PORCH - p. 38

Spending time in nature is beautiful and amazing, especially on a clear crisp day. Sometimes when I'm feeling lost, out of sorts, or simply need to unwind, I sit on my porch in silence with my dog on my lap and take in all my splendid surroundings, in awe that I am even allowed this view.

GOOD MORNING SUNSHINE - p. 45

I don't think I had ever seen a sunrise before this poem was conceived. If I had, it wasn't memorable.

I was on a Disney cruise, which is magical enough, and decided to wake up to see the sun rise over the ocean. If you know me, you know this in and of itself is a miracle, because I don't do dawn o'clock, ever. I'm just not an early morning person, unless pulling an all-nighter, which is fathomable for me.

My brother, family friend Tom and I made the plan to meet on the deck at the appointed time. I struggled to get up, but I made it, and was so glad I did. The spectacle had me hypnotized. I was, and still am amazed by the sun's magnificence and persistence.

Watching the sun rise from where I live now doesn't evoke the same emotions, though I am truly grateful for each morning. You kind of have to be on a cruise, or near a body of water, or on a wide-open plain that's unencumbered by buildings or vegetation to devour the full experience. Seeing the sun rise is breathtaking with the array of colors, the blinding brightness, and the pure elicitation of joy. Knowing that with each rotation you are offered a new opportunity.

Now, whenever I'm on a cruise, I make a point of waking up with the sun, just to greet it and be amazed all over again. And not once have I been disappointed. In my opinion, this should be on everyone's bucket list. It's a freebie that will give you a jolt of bliss.

Read *Kissed* - p. 74. It's another tribute to the beauty of nature, written about the bliss I felt waking up alive and healthy on one of my birthdays.

GOODBYE TO EVERYTHING - p. 46

This poem was inspired by a multitude of major metamorphoses. Many changes were taking place in my life simultaneously – a couple of long term friendships expired, a position that I had enjoyed for a year 'blossomed' into a nightmare, a relationship that needed to end long ago was punctuated by a relocation, and to top it all off, I found out that my father, whom I had chosen to blame my poor relationship decisions on, was diagnosed with a terminal illness and didn't have long to live.

I had known for years that my one friend lied to get out of simple stuff, it was just what she did. I knew that when I was going through the roughest period in my life, she lied to get me out her house. The lie was so dumb and silly sounding, I knew it was a lie at the time, but my life was so broken that I didn't have the energy to concentrate on her or the lie, I just had to find somewhere else to live. This event wasn't the end, though. It was just one of the main reasons that aided in the decision to back out of our friendship when I finally had enough.

I had always had an on-again, off-again relationship with the friend who confirmed the previous friend's lie. Always! We would be the best of friends for years and then out of the blue we would ghost one another for years, without fighting or arguing. It was the weirdest thing.

I can't speak as to why she ghosted me because we never discussed our breakups during the on-again periods. But the last time I ghosted her was a combination of her telling me about the other friend's lie and me tiring of the rollercoaster ride. I felt she had been trying to be a wedge in my relationship with the first friend for years, though I have no evidence to support this, just a feeling, adding up different things. For one, she had no reason to tell me about the first friend's lie. I never asked if she knew anything about the situation, although I did discuss what happened with her.

Then there was the job situation. It was good until it wasn't. I really think it was God telling me not to get too comfortable, because the 'kindness to chaos' of it all was just too complex to be anything else.

And the guy that I needed to move on from, up and moved, out of the blue. Which it turns out, was another blessing because God knew I would have never exited that go-no-where, good-for-nothing but sex 'relationship' otherwise.

And then there was dad. Now I know he did the best he knew how to do with the tools he was given. How I wish I could have embodied this knowledge and forged new ways of relating to males a long time ago. What I did instead is that as relationship after relationship failed, I needed someone to blame my poor choices on. And of course, I wasn't going to take the blame. So, I handed that torch to my dad. Which is the worst thing I could have done because not only did it incumber the relationship I could have had with him, it also allowed me to continue making poor decisions in his name.

His death punctuated all that. And I was left with a world of regret, still having to figure out how to navigate relationships. What I discovered is I didn't know how to love myself, how to set healthy boundaries, and mostly how to walk away when it doesn't feel like what I need it to feel like.

What I learned is that everybody's journey is different so what I'm about to say may not work in your life but it sure won't hurt. Procrastination is not good unless you're procrastinating about doing something bad or detrimental. I say this because all these major events didn't have to happen at the same time had I dealt with them in turn, when I felt the first inkling that something was out of alignment. Granted, you're not always aware of the whys, but when you first know, act. Because you never want to have to deal with all these major events at the same time, like I did. It's much easier to tackle them head on. Most of the time if you allow something to fester, it will become bigger and harder to deal with. So, boss up and put that period at the end of the sentence now.

There is a freedom in goodbye.

Everything Is Temporary - p. 33 was written in the midst of my separation, shortly after I moved in with the friend I discussed above. I was truly going through some desperate times. But this is a poem of hope. *My Beautiful Surrender* - p. 86 and *Think it Through* - p. 115, were also written during this tumultuous time.

I BELIEVED YOU - p. 55

This is a love poem to my dad. I wrote it shortly after he passed.

We didn't have the relationship I craved, but all that wishing is done now. I saw him struggle to tell me that 'he always loved me,' gasping for breath because of COPD brought on by a lifetime of smoking cigarettes. I felt every single one of those words, his last to me. And that simple phrase helped heal a lifetime of hurt.

I STILL LOVE - p. 58

Have you ever met the right person at the wrong time? That's what this poem is all about.

It starts off telling the reader what was 'said' to me as the relationship was ending. Then, it transitions to me reminiscing about her, about us, and thinking how much I still, to this day, wish I had been ready.

We're still 'friends' and occasionally keep in contact through social media. She is married now and expecting. Every time she posts a pic of her new life, pings of jealousy swarm my entire body, knowing how good we could have been together.

Every dream we discussed, she is living while, at the time I conceived this poem, I was still stuck in the same ole life I had when I was with her, same deadbeat relationship, same dreaded job, same dull life. Just looking at all the dreams she had checked off helped me make moves, live life differently, be better. And she doesn't even know that she's still attributing to my success.

Another related poem is *Popcorn Ceilings* - p. 100.

I'M HOT - p. 61
Hot flashes are a real thing, in case you didn't know it or have yet to live through one. They are rare for me but when they hit, they knock me slam off my feet.

The particular one I wrote about in this poem happened at a movie theater while watching the latest incarnation of the Matt Damon, *Bourne* series, with my mom. My mom was laughing, maybe she was having a flash herself, a flashback. Or maybe she was just ecstatic she no longer had them. But nothing at all was funny. I was miserable!

If you love consuming hot flash verses and need another poem on this topic, read *Eve & Apples* - p. 32.

IT WAS A WOMAN - p. 66

This poem was written as a tribute to my mother and all the mothers of the world. Who would we be without their tireless energy?

My mom went to college in her late twenties, while raising two bratty kids alone. And although I knew she was in school, I swear I don't ever recall her missing a beat with us. I couldn't have done it. I barely can find time now, working, just caring for myself and the dog.

Thank you, Mom.

IT'S OVER NOW - p. 67

This is by far one of the favorite poems I have written.

In the immortal words of The Temptation's, *Papa Was a Rollin' Stone,* it was the third of September. That day I'll always remember …, …that was the day my daddy died.

My relationship with my daddy could be described as slim and none. He wasn't bad, he wasn't good. I barely 'knew' him at all. In fact, I've learned more about my father since his death than I ever knew while he lived. Admittedly, I have some responsibility in our lack of relationship.

This poem was written thinking about our relationship but as I wrote, I thought about all the animus relationships I have had over the years and I could replace my dad with any of these folks and the poem would have the same meaning. Get over it now. It's not worth it. That's what's important.

Granted, I'm sure my dad regretted our lack of a relationship, but what I learned and what you need to hear is that concentrating on it, letting the toxic feelings fester, won't hurt anyone but you. They'll go one living their lives, unaware that you are or have been weary. Life is too short to hang on to these feelings. Wasting even another second filtering other relationships through your hurts is a mistake. Do whatever you have to do to heal, because time is not on your side.

It wasn't until my daddy's death that I was able to begin my healing. I was damn near fifty years old. Imagine, imagine what I could have done with all that time, all that wasted angst.

LEMONADE - p. 76

My grandfather was a very quiet and reserved, brilliant man. And I was way too busy doing nothing to notice or draw information about his life from him. In case you don't get it, this is my way of telling you how selfish I was.

This poem was written about a trip our family took to DC. This was an 'event'! I don't recall ever traveling with my grandparents, ever.

My Grandfather's nephew is a lawyer who had worked in the Clinton administration, which is beside the point. His sister from California, was visiting her son and his family. And since she was so close, considering, we decided to take him to see her. And though they all were more than kind, I was intimidated. One of the nephew's teenage sons was on a road trip tour of the Civil Rights south. This blew my mind. 'Who are these people?' was all I could think.

My grandpa had two sisters, Sarah and Winifred, whom I had never met before this luncheon. As my grandpa and his sister Winifred talked for hours, I sat quiet like a little kid who wasn't allowed to speak around grown folk. I'll never forget this moment. And there I was, with my uncouth self, trying not to drink up all the lemonade, while soaking up everything they were talking about.

MAYBE NOT - p. 81

Me trying to decide whether or not to get involved in a new relationship.

NEW ME - p. 89

Chile, I had a broken picker, always choosing cheaters, liars, and damaged people. For most of my adult life if you liked me, I'd roll the dice if I was attracted to you (yep, this used to be 'THE' only requirement). I'm not too far out of that way of being and I'm a grown ass woman.

This poem is about my fear of making another bad decision. After I finally realized what I was doing wrong, it took me a while to jump back out into the dating game. Not sure if aloneness would allow me to do the same thing once again.

I finally got my picker fixed and am now confident that I will make the best choice for me. In fact, I was recently introduced to a man that I was so attracted to. I know for sure he would have rocked my world in the bed, and even worse, uprooted my peace. And now that I know me, peace is something I'm not willing to compromise, for nobody!

A poem with the same sentiment is *Precious Peace* - p. 102.

THE SHIRT - p. 108
This poem is a love psalm to my grandma, Petunia.

THE SUN WILL SHINE AGAIN - p. 112
I was in shambles when Michael Jackson passed. I really took it hard like he was family. I didn't know I loved MJ like that. Maybe it was the tragic circumstances, but it took me about two weeks to get back to some semblance of normality.

And then there was Prince. I struggled the day he died. This poem was born because of his passing. At the time, it felt like there was so much noise around me. I couldn't get my peace from all the usual ways. So, I took the dog and the fold up chair and sat outside in the driveway and wrote this, staring into the clouds.

SWEET SAX - p. 114
When we get back to normal you've got to see saxophonist Marcus Anderson perform live. It will change your life and have you thinking he's proposing to you. He navigates the venue like a gifted hypnotist, seducing with his sax.

THERE, THEIR, THEY'RE - p. 115

Okay, I'll admit it, the last English class I took was in the early 1990s, almost three decades ago. And I have not written any work of length since then, until I set out to write my first novel, *Do You Really Know Camille?*

Suffice it to say, I had a rough go of it. Using picture when I meant pitcher, and weather instead of whether. And had I not hired someone to read the book, I would have never realized my mistakes. The editing of my novel inspired this poem.

WHERE WE LEFT IT - p. 132

College in the 90s was everything. I met my best friend from UNC because we were the only two black girls in Everett dorm. We were inseparable for years, before cell phones.

She went off to Law school in DC after graduation, I stayed in NC. And although we didn't see each other as much, we still talked on the phone every single day. We didn't see the wedges forming between us, but slowly over time, especially after we met significant others, we stopped communicating as often. Unless you have an Oprah/Gayle friendship, this separation is a normal progression of life.

We both married, she had kids and life went on. Now, If I hear her voice once a year, that's a lot.

When the National Museum of African American History and Culture opened in DC I had to go. Another friend obtained the coveted tickets and we were off. My college friend graciously let us stay with her and her family. Our visit with her during this trip was the inspiration for this poem.

YOUR WORST ENEMY - p. 137

This may not be the case in your life, but what I have found in my five decades, is that most of the problems and troubles that I have encountered, I actively participated in and/or invited into my life. And this is what this poem is all about.

I implore you to look at the burdensome situations you find yourself in and ask if you had a hand in what is happening, by your poor choices or inaction. If the answer is yes, don't beat yourself up, just work hard to choose better.

A similar poem is *Blame Game* - p. 10.

www.ingramcontent.com/pod-product-compliance
Lightning Source LLC
Chambersburg PA
CBHW022107090426
42743CB00008B/748